W9-AAI-949

Wizards and Wishes

Kathleen B. Hester

Joanne Boehm

LAIDLAW BROTHERS • PUBLISHERS

A Division of Doubleday & Company, Inc.

RIVER FOREST, ILLINOIS

Irvine, California   Chamblee, Georgia   Dallas, Texas   Toronto, Canada

Acknowledgments

Atheneum Publishers, Inc. for "Tug of War" by Kathleen Fraser. Copyright © 1968 by Kathleen Fraser from STILTS, SOMERSAULTS AND HEADSTANDS used by permission of Atheneum Publishers.

Boys' Life Magazine for "Searching for the Loch Ness Monster" by Mary Fiore. Reprinted by permission of the author and BOYS' LIFE, published by the Boy Scouts of America.

Eve Bunting for "Once There Was a Pier." Used by permission of Eve Bunting.

(Acknowledgments continued on page 264.)

Project Director Shirley Graudin / *Supervising Editor* Janette Pralle Marcus / *Staff Editors* Mary Lou Beilfuss Byrne, Olga Tamara Popowych / *Production Director* LaVergne G. Niequist / *Coordinator of Production* Terese M. Lyons / *Production Supervisor* Mary C. Steermann / *Production Associate* Anthony Giometti / *Production Assistant* M. Catherine Linne / *Photo Researcher* William A. Cassin / *Art Director* Gloria Muczynski / *Assistants to the Art Director* Emily Fina Friel, Dennis Horan / *Cover and Title Page Art* Tak Murakami / *Cover photograph by* Edward Hoppe

Illustrators   Shirley Beckes, 261–262; Corinne and Robert Borja, 3–7; George Hamblin, 19–20, 232–233; Pat and Paul Karch, 241–246; David Kingham, 198–203; Bob Korta, 235–239, 240; Gordon Laite, 44–57; Michael Lowenbein, 164–169; Linda Maddelena, 58–59; Dick Martin, 60, 105, 163, 209, 263; Robert Masheris, 99–100, 155–160, 161; Joan McGurren, 154; Donald C. Meighan, 28–29, 38, 40–41, 63, 104, 206–207, 227; Keith Neeley, 218–219, 247–248; Tom O'Sullivan, 122–144; Al Pucci, 8–18, 210–217; Sandy Rabinowitz, 220–225; Jack Reilly, 21, 69, 106–110, 146–147; Joe Rogers, 145, 195–197, 259–260; Monica Santa, 42–43, 148–153; Rex Schneider, 120–121; Miriam Schottland, 114–119; Bill Shires, 22–27; Sam Sirdofsky, 208; Ray Skibinski, 174–194; David Stone, 72–89; George Ulrich, 170–172; Jack Wallen, 90–91, 112–113, 204–205

Photographers   Ed Hoppe Photography, 41, 68, 226; Artstreet, 31; Lee Boltin, 253 (inset), 255 (both), 259 (left and right); Devaney, 95; Leo de Wys Inc., 93; Tim Dinsdale, 30; EPA, 173; Robert Harding Picture Library, 250 (left), 257 (top and inset); Vance Henry/Taurus, 259 (middle); F.L. Kenett/Robert Harding Picture Library, 250 (right); Jack Kerber, 61, 67, 101–103; Steve McCutcheon, 228, 229; Metropolitan Museum of Art, 253, 257 (bottom), 258 (top); William S. Nawrocki, 109, 111; Photo Stock Library, 32, 39; Photri, 249, 254, 258 (bottom); Walter Rawlings/Photri, 110; Road Rider Magazine, 70, 71; Louise Scherbyn, 96–98; Tom Stack & Associates, 34, 36, 92; George Miksch Sutton for the Ornithology Laboratory, Cornell University, 234 (top); Reprinted by permission of Tribune Company Syndicate, Inc., 162 (cartoon); Paintings "Bald Eagle" and "Wild Geese" by George Miksch Sutton used courtesy of World Book, Inc., 234

ISBN 0-8445-0606-0

Copyright © 1984 by
Laidlaw Brothers, Publishers
A Division of Doubleday & Company, Inc.

CONTENTS

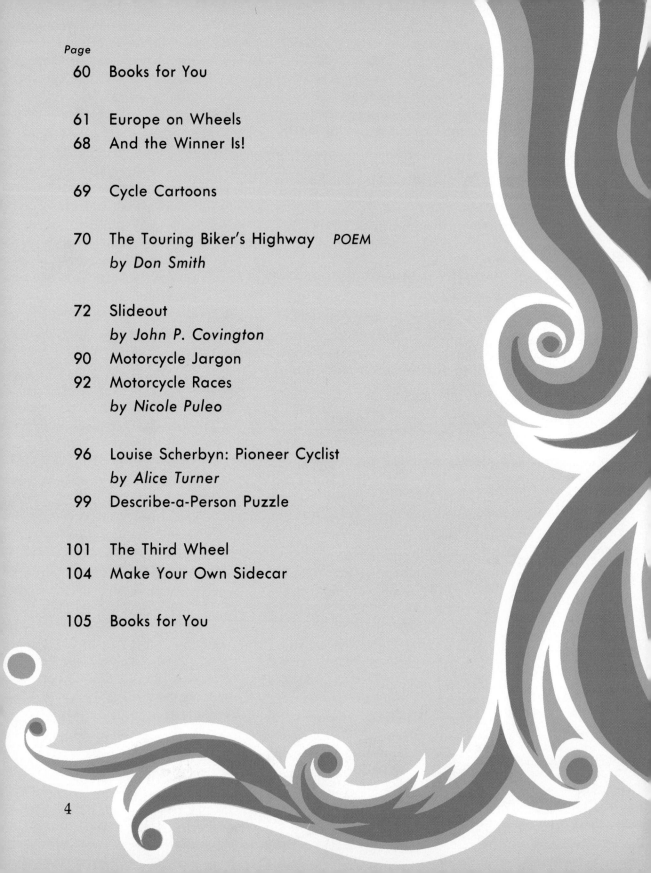

Sasquatch:
Creature of the North
by Casey Callahan

The two men were talking quietly when the secretary walked in. She placed a folder marked TOP SECRET on the Director's desk. "Sir, this just came from the White House."

The Director thanked her and waited until she left the room. He swiftly picked up the folder. Inside, he found three small photographs. The Director looked at them for what seemed like a long time. Then he slowly handed them over to Special Agent Tom Whiteclaw.

"This is your next job, Tom. Study these photographs for a moment, and tell me what you think."

Agent Whiteclaw quickly glanced at the three photographs. A confused look crossed his face. "Why should the government be interested in pictures of a giant ape?"

The Director rose and walked over to a large picture window. He looked out over the Potomac River. In a quiet voice he said, "It is not quite an ape, Tom."

Agent Whiteclaw watched the Director fold and unfold his hands several times, as if he were trying to keep the tension from entering his voice.

"Tom, the creature you are looking at is almost seven feet tall. A rough guess of its weight would be in the neighborhood of four hundred pounds. Look closely at the photographs. You'll notice that the face, hands, and feet are not covered with hair." The Director turned away from the window and stared at Special Agent Whiteclaw. "Tom," he whispered, "that creature has the face of a human."

Tom felt a wave of fear flash through his body. He recalled old tribal legends that he had heard from his grandfather—legends about the giant creatures of the North. Tom searched his mind for the Indian name his grandfather had used to describe them. "Sasquatch," he recalled, shuddering a little. Tom's ancestors used to talk about the many battles between the giant creatures and the Indians, and how the Sasquatch were neither animal nor Indian. It was something few white poeple knew about.

The Director's voice brought Tom out of the hidden past and back into the office. "As you know, Tom, one of the cabinet members has not yet returned from his fishing trip. We sent out a small search party, and they found his camp." Lowering his eyes for a moment, the Director continued, "The search party reported that the camp was wrecked. There was some blood on the ground and several strands of long, matted hair. Nothing else except for a camera, which is how we came into possession of these photographs."

The Director poured two cups of coffee. "Tom," he said, "the President wants to know what happened to the missing cabinet secretary. He especially wants to know if this is the work of enemy agents. By this time tomorrow night, you should be deep in the forests of the Pacific Northwest."

Twenty-four hours later, Tom looked at his watch. Right on time, he thought. He bent over and removed the parachute from his pet wolf, Lupe. Lupe's ancestors and Tom's ancestors had once hunted each other. Now, the wolf was almost extinct—and Tom's tribe was growing smaller. The bond between the man and the wolf was strong. Now they were going to seek a third creature—the likes of which neither had seen before.

"Come on, Lupe," Tom said. "I want to get to the cabinet secretary's camp before dark. Maybe we can pick up a few clues there."

Tom and Lupe began climbing the steep mountain. Tom was in good shape, but the thin mountain air and the heavy backpack began to slow him down. He paused

for a moment to gaze at the beauty of a raging waterfall. Spray from the falls fell very gently upon his forehead.

While Tom stopped to rest a moment, Lupe went on up the steep trail. As always, Lupe tested the wind for scent. Not finding any, he began a sweeping search of the ground. He discovered a faint scent that he didn't recognize. It was not the light smell of the deer, nor was it the strong smell of the bear. It was something very different, something very unpleasant. It made Lupe nervous.

Together, Tom and the wolf reached the top. After quickly setting up camp, Tom stopped to look around.

Night falls swiftly in the high mountain forests. One moment it was dusk—and the next, pitch dark. Tom couldn't even see the huge storm clouds rolling across the sky. The clouds covered the high mountains, creating a thick fog. Tom and Lupe crouched close together in front of the small campfire to keep warm.

Suddenly, Lupe sensed something. It was the strange scent that he had discovered earlier. This time it was stronger—and closer. It was coming their way, heading directly for the camp. Lupe growled. Tom looked at Lupe and pulled a burning torch from the fire to light the area. Lupe kept up his low-keyed growling and fixed a stare at a spot in the fog. Tom listened for the slightest sound. Nothing. He held Lupe's mouth to silence him. Still nothing. Lupe shivered. He panicked and tried to break away from Tom.

"Easy, Lupe. I don't want you to get hurt by whatever is out there."

Lupe started struggling, trying to charge into the fog. Suddenly, with a burst of strength, he broke away from Tom.

Tom whirled to grab Lupe, and then, what he saw almost paralyzed him with fear. Framed in the shadows of the fog was the giant Sasquatch.

The creature was coming toward them. Tom held his
torch high. Lupe had stopped dead in his tracks. The
creature appeared enraged, but he feared the fire that
Tom held in his hands. Sasquatch stopped.

Tom had been well trained. He fought the panic that
raced through his body. He knew that the creature's huge
arms could rip him apart in a moment. His life depended
upon the small torch he held in his hands.

Holding up the torch, Tom bent over and grabbed Lupe. Slowly, very slowly, he backed away from Sasquatch until he was on the edge of the cliff. Above the roar of the falls he could hear grumbling, growling sounds.

For what seemed like forever, the two enemies faced each other. The eyes of Sasquatch watched as Tom's torch flickered in the wind. As the flame died down, the creature became more enraged. It opened its mouth, and two long teeth shone in the dying firelight. The creature started to move, very slowly at first. It circled to the right, moving away from the campfire.

Tom's mind was working quickly. His campfire was now ashes, and he could feel the heat from the torch as the small flame rapidly ate at the stick he was holding. The creature was in a terrible rage, but it was holding itself back. It seemed to know that soon this human would be quite defenseless.

Somewhere below on the valley floor, the forces of nature started to gather. Strong winds spun up through the canyons, gathering in strength. Without warning, the wind brushed past Agent Whiteclaw, putting out his torch. At the same moment, Tom decided that he must take Sasquatch by surprise.

With a mighty cry, Tom charged at the creature. Lupe joined in the attack. For a split second, Tom felt himself being picked up, but he was quickly dropped when the full weight of Lupe landed on the creature. Lupe was everywhere at once. The two battled fiercely, but Sasquatch was unable to match Lupe's swift movements. Although the creature had the strength of ten people, its huge build made it slow and clumsy. It was a fight that

had undoubtedly taken place before in nature. Lupe's ancestors had passed on to him the knowledge that speed and repeated attack are necessary for survival.

Tom was given a short rest as Lupe drove Sasquatch to the ground. Lupe was everywhere, snapping and biting with all his strength. He never stayed in one spot long enough for the creature to grab him.

Tom came to Lupe's aid. He grabbed a handful of burning ashes and threw them at Sasquatch. The creature, startled, rolled backward. Without warning, the thin cliff edge gave way. The creature tumbled down the hollow and into the raging river and was swiftly swallowed by the rushing waters.

"And so, sir, Lupe and I searched all the following day, but we were unable to find the creature's remains. I think that the current probably carried the body out to sea."

Tom handed his written report to the Director. "You'll notice, sir, that my report states merely that I did not uncover any clues as to what happened to the secretary. But I have no doubt that he fell victim to Sasquatch. There is no reason to believe it was enemy agents."

Far off in the Pacific Northwest, at an area near where the sea meets the river, a doe and her two fawns were drinking from a quiet pool. The doe noticed a thick log that floated in the pool. The soft current carried the log to the forested shoreline. To the doe's surprise, the log started to move. She signaled her two fawns, and they ran into the brush. Pausing for one last look, the doe watched the log crawl slowly into the forest, heading in the direction of the mountains.

Agent Whiteclaw's Special Report

Imagine that you are Special Agent Tom Whiteclaw. You have to write a report of your trip for the Director to send to the White House. A good reporter tells facts only. He or she does not include personal feelings or ideas in the report. Yet you know that what the doe saw should be on record, and you have some ideas about what should be done next.

After talking with the Director, you decide to write a factual report. But you will add a secret report telling what you think about the giant creature at the end. In that way the Director will have some evidence to use when he makes future plans to catch the giant creature.

To write the report you need to do two things. First, write a factual report of your experiences. Then write the secret report, using a code.

To write the factual report, do these things:
- Make a list of the most important happenings in the story. You may include the following:
    - Your interview with the Director
    - Your arrival in the Pacific Northwest
    - Your encounter with Sasquatch
    - The search for its body
- Select important details that will expand the most important points.
- Write the report clearly and neatly.

To write the secret part of the report, use this code. It is a diagram drawn like tick-tack-toe.

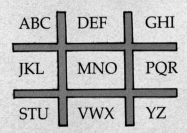

ABC	DEF	GHI
JKL	MNO	PQR
STU	VWX	YZ

To decode the message below, do these things:

• Find the correct two-, three-, or four-sided box in the diagram above.
• If there is no dot, it is the first letter in that box.
• If there is one dot, it is the second letter in that box.
• If there are two dots, it is the third letter in that box. For example, the first word in the message is *I*.

What is the message?

Now write the secret part of the report, using the code above.

• Think of what you are going to write in the secret report. For example, do you think the giant creature may have died? Tell why or why not. Tell what future plans should be made.
• Write your ideas and suggestions, using the secret code. Choose a friend to act as Director and give your report to him or to her to read.

Good work, Special Agent Whiteclaw!

Monster Amusements

Q. What do you call the land where monsters live?
A. A terror-tory.

Q. What sort of beans does a werewolf like?
A. Human beans.

Q. What do you call a monster who goes to school?
A. A student.

Q. What do you say when you meet a two-headed monster?
A. "Hello, hello. How are you? How are you?"

Q. What do monsters do every morning at 10:30?
A. Take a coffin break.

Q. What do you do with a blue monster?
A. Cheer him up.

Q. How do you make a sea-monster float?
A. Fill a glass half full of root beer; then add two
    scoops of ice cream and a sea monster.

THIS WAY to Monsters

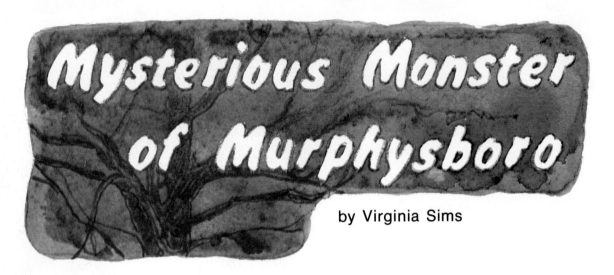

Mysterious Monster of Murphysboro

by Virginia Sims

How do you feel about monsters? Not the one-eyed types that glare at you from behind the safety of your television screens. But the kind reported in newspapers every once in a while. The kind everyday people—minding their own business—vow up and down they've seen.

Like the lonely herder in Nepal, who comes panting in with a report about an "Abominable Snowman," the huge Yeti that's supposed to prowl the slopes of the Himalayas. Or the Pacific Northwest logger, who claims he saw Bigfoot—Sasquatch, the Indians called it—and points out a giant twenty-inch footprint to prove it. Or the Scottish fisherman who stares in disbelief as a great slithering form, longer than a boxcar, rises from the black waters of Loch Ness.

Are you a believer in monsters? A disbeliever? Well, in either case, come along and meet a couple of kids who met one. They are Randy Creath and Cheryl Ray, who live in the quiet little southern Illinois town of Murphysboro on the banks of the Big Muddy River. Both were in their fourth year at Murphysboro Township High. And for them it all began on a warm evening one summer.

"It was about 10 o'clock at night, and I'd just taken Cheryl home," Randy said. "We were sitting there on her back porch talking when we heard something moving in the trees and brush about fifty feet away. I threw some rocks, and nothing happened. So we started down to have a look."

"I was about twenty or thirty feet behind Randy," Cheryl recalled, "but we both saw it about the same time— something big and kind of white coming through the weeds. I ran back to turn on the porch light. And I told my mother that something was out there. She called the police, and I went back to where Randy was. By that time, Randy had nearly reached the clump of bushes. Suddenly, we both froze."

"It was just standing there—this huge, strange-looking thing. It was at least seven feet tall—maybe taller. It had dirty-white or cream-colored hair all over it, as far as I could tell. The night was dark, and I could not see its face. But Cheryl thought she could," Randy said.

"Well, all I could see were its eyes," Cheryl added. "They were red and round, and they kind of glowed. They reminded me of cats' eyes. It stood tall—not hunched over like an ape. And its arms hung straight down so that its hands were into the brush. You couldn't see if it had any claws. And it smelled just awful."

For a minute or two, the kids and the creature stood about fifteen feet apart staring at one another. Then the creature turned and crashed through

the bushes toward the river, which is about a half mile cross-country from Cheryl's house.

"I followed it a little way," said Randy, "but it made so much noise that I thought there might be two of them. So I went back to the house."

The night was far from over. The police already had been warned that some strange something might be prowling about. Several nights before, a frightened couple had reported that they had heard a hair-raising noise and had spotted a huge light-colored creature near the town's boat dock. The police had found some strange-looking footprints in the river mud.

When the police arrived at Cheryl's house, they were ready for a real search. They brought along a tracking dog, which followed a rough path of broken branches and globs of slime. The slime was very much like sludge from the sewage-treatment plant, which lies between the house and the river. The path led to a deserted barn on a neighboring farm. But when the dog got to the barn door, it backed off, whined, and refused to go in. Police cars with spotlights were called into the area. But when the police entered the barn, it was empty.

The creature appeared just one more time. In the middle
of the night about a week later, some ponies that were part
of a traveling carnival began to whinny and shy and try to
pull free from their ropes. Carnival workers checking the
uproar saw a huge, whitish creature standing in the bushes.
It wasn't moving. It just stood there, its head cocked,
watching the ponies. The carnival workers ran for help, but
when they returned, the creature was gone.

That was enough to make "monster believers" out of
the whole town of Murphysboro. The town officials asked
for the advice of Harlan Sorkin of St. Louis, Missouri, who
has made a study of such monster sightings. He told the
officials that the descriptions of the Murphysboro monster
matched those of over 300 other sightings in

North America during the past ten years. He called the monster by the old Indian name of Sasquatch—a creature, he said, that is believed to eat underwater plants and live in river caves. That spring's high flooding, he thought, might have driven it from its home. He described the creature as usually very shy and peaceful, but having great strength and speed when frightened or attacked. But that, of course, is just one person's view.

Since that summer of 1974, Murphysboro has had more than its share of curiosity seekers. "And," adds Randy, "there was a rumor going around that somebody shot a big white bear down south somewhere—and that that was what we saw. Well, I know what bears look like, and it wasn't any bear. And it certainly wasn't an ape. I never heard of one that big—and it wasn't even built like an ape."

When asked how it feels to share your neighborhood with a monster, Cheryl and Randy admitted to being a little uneasy.

"But," Randy added, "the creature has never been known to attack a human—and it didn't hurt anybody here. I just wish everybody would leave it alone. It's got a place in nature, too."

Sand Casting

Some people who claim to have seen Sasquatch or Bigfoot have preserved the monster's footprint to prove that claim. On these two pages are directions for preserving your own footprint, using plaster and sand.

Materials: sand, plaster of Paris, a mixing bowl, a shoe box, water, a soft brush, a spoon.

Step 1

Pour sand into the box, leaving ½ inch of unfilled space at the top of the box. Add water until the sand is firm but not runny. Use your hand or a piece of cardboard to level the sand in the box.

Step 2

Press your foot firmly into the sand. Remove your foot carefully so that your footprint is set firmly and is clearly outlined.

Step 3

Mix the plaster of Paris. Put the water in the mixing bowl first. Then add the plaster of Paris. Otherwise the water and the plaster of Paris won't mix properly. You will need about 2½ cups of water and 3½ to 4 cups of plaster of Paris. Stir until the mixture looks and feels like heavy cream. Use a spoon or a stick. If the mixture is too runny, add a little more plaster of Paris. The plaster should be used at once because it sets quickly.

Step 4

Carefully spoon the plaster into the box, filling all the footprint first. If plaster is poured from the bowl into the box, the weight will break down the footprint you have made. So it must be added carefully. After all the footprint has been filled and a thin layer of plaster covers the sand, the rest of the plaster may be poured carefully into the box.

Level the plaster with a piece of cardboard.

Step 5

Allow the plaster to dry for an hour. Loosen the sides of the box and remove your plaster cast. Place it right side up and let it dry for another half hour.

Step 6

Take the soft brush. Gently brush the surface to remove the extra sand.

Remaining sand in the shoe box may be used over and over again.

Searching for the Loch Ness Monster

by Mary Fiore

The clock in the 200-year-old church tower near Foyers, Scotland, had just struck nine on the morning of April 23, 1960. For Tim Dinsdale, standing with his movie camera on the shore of Loch Ness, it was the most exciting hour of the most important day in his life. Seconds before, Dinsdale had sighted the Loch Ness monster swimming in the loch off Foyers. Now, as the old clock rang the hour, Tim was filming the monster in the water.

The excitement was almost unbearable. Tim was capturing a legend on film—a legend that had begun back in the sixth century. Perhaps Tim's film would prove that there really is a monster, a strange, unknown creature living in the loch (the Gaelic word for *lake*) in northern Scotland.

Suddenly, the monster submerged. Dinsdale waited a few moments to be certain the creature would not surface again. Then he jumped into his car and drove off to have the film developed.

When developed, those few feet of film changed Dinsdale's way of life and began a new stage in the hunt for "Nessie"—as the monster is called. The film was one of the main reasons that the Loch Ness Phenomena Investigation Bureau was formed in 1961. The purpose of the Bureau is to record all searches and keep track of the growing list of sightings.

The Loch Ness monster is said to have been first sighted in the sixth century. In the centuries since, there have been more than 3,000 reported sightings of Nessie! Firsthand reports describe her as an ugly, shy, greenish-black creature, from five to sixty feet long and from one to five feet wide. She is said to have a snakelike head, a long neck, and a wide, flat body with from one to seven camellike humps. Some say she looks like a dinosaur.

Universities around the world have sent teams either to find the monster or to kill the legend. To date, Nessie has eluded them all.

A few years ago I was a member of one of those teams. Our group went to Drumnadrochit, a tiny town midway down the twenty-four-mile-long Loch Ness. There we set up headquarters for two weeks while we tried to find Nessie—or at least find out more about her.

Loch Ness is a spectacular sight. It is a mile wide and about 700 feet deep. In some places, though, it is over 1,000 feet deep, more than the height of a ninety-story building. The loch is surrounded by cliffs and hills. From the high roads around it, the water looks blue and clear.

From lakeside, it is neither. The almost-black water has so much peat that at fewer than 20 feet down, divers have trouble seeing anything. The icy water can be mirror-smooth or splash up eight-foot waves at a moment's notice. Winds up to 100 miles an hour are not rare. The morning and evening mists add to the loch's spookiness. All in all, if a family of monsters were looking for a home, Loch Ness would be the best choice.

Scientists believe that, from 5,000 to 10,000 years ago, Loch Ness was part of the North Sea. During a shifting of sea level caused by meltings at the end of the Ice Age, the loch was cut off from the sea by a narrow strip of land. At that time many creatures—both male and female—were trapped in it. These creatures, scientists believe, may have lived through the ages. So, the Loch Ness monster is most likely not one, but a family of monsters.

Every day our group would report to Temple Pier, the lakeside headquarters for the Underwater Division of the Loch Ness Phenomena Investigation Bureau. The Bureau records the growing list of monster sightings, accepting only those it feels are unquestionable. More sightings are rejected than are accepted. Any made thirty minutes before or after a boat passes an area are rejected. The loch is so calm at times that a ship's wake can ripple for a full half hour after the ship has passed. The bureau is anxious not to confuse a ship's wake with a Nessie sighting.

All the workers at the bureau are serious about finding Nessie. Perhaps the most serious is Tim Dinsdale, who reportedly gave up a very good job with an airplane company to head the Bureau's Surface Division. This, of course, was after he took his spectacular film of the monster swimming in the loch. I have seen Tim's film, and to see it is to know that a monster exists. The film shows a creature with a head and neck about six feet above the water, swimming away from where Tim was standing. When a bus (which is visible in the film) went by on the other shore, the monster, probably frightened by the motor's noise, turned and swam back toward Tim's camera. Then the monster submerged, leaving only a foamy wake.

While I was there, the Bureau's Underwater Division was headed by an American, Robert Love. Love and a group of divers from England were trying to raise the wreck of a hundred-year-old sailing ship discovered on a ledge, 100 feet down in the loch. The boat was found in 1969 by a small submarine brought to the lake to hunt Nessie.

One day I was at the pier when the divers came up from their work on the ship. As the first diver surfaced, I sensed something had happened. He tore the air hose from his mouth and yelled, "I stepped on something!" Seconds later the other diver bobbed to the surface and shouted the same thing. Both quickly swam the 200 feet to shore.

"What do you think you stepped on?" I asked.

"I don't know," one diver answered, "but whatever it was, it was big!"

A group of scientists from Massachusetts were at the pier that day, using a far-out method to find Nessie. They put lures of powerful-smelling fish oils in the water, different scents to attract males and females. They also coated three buoys with the scents and put them into the loch. (The buoys later disappeared and have not been seen since.) The smell of the lures was awful, something only a creature like Nessie could love.

The Massachusetts group had its own sonar equipment for underwater tracking to monitor the area where it had put the lures. It was in this area that the divers "stepped on something."

As I was talking to the divers, one of the scientists rushed from the sonar shed and asked if they had seen anything, because the sonar had picked up something big in the area. One diver answered, "I was just starting up when my foot pushed against something solid. It really got me up fast!"

Could the divers have brushed against each other or against the mast of the ship? They decided they were too far apart to have hit each other and thought it too much of a coincidence that they both hit the mast. "I'd like to think it was Nessie," said one of the divers, "but then again, I'm not so sure. I've got to go down again tomorrow."

Each diver carried a long knife in a sheath below his right knee. A knife would probably not be used on Nessie unless it was a matter of life or death, because she is protected by British law. Both a fine and a prison term are possible for anyone who harms her. There is a reward for finding Nessie, but it is payable only if she is alive and well.

Among our own group's equipment, one of the most interesting pieces was an infrared camera for photographing in total darkness. The camera was used because 80 percent of all sightings of Nessie have taken place at dawn.

Each morning at four, two members of our group made a sonar-boat run of the lake. On my turn, a particularly chilly night, I dressed quickly. Temple Pier was black, silent, and spooky as we tiptoed past the trailers. We did not want to wake those Underwater Bureau members who were not coming on the run. The shore area at the pier had been lined with lights just under the water, and they gave off a greenish glow.

During the run, I sat in the cabin and watched the sonar equipment. Sonar shows everything in its path, from small salmon to caves along the shoreline. Studies showed that whenever Nessie was caught on the sonar, all fish in the area disappeared. Whether they were frightened—or eaten by Nessie—remains to be seen. When Nessie disappeared from the screen, it was assumed that she swam into a cave.

We had no luck on my run. But the following night, while the two team members were waiting to board the boat, one of the lights under the water's surface at the pier began to do a strange dance. Down, down the light went, then up, as if it were caught on something that was trying to shake it loose. Finally, the light came loose and floated to the surface—ripped from its bracket. Was it caught on Nessie? The two men on the sonar run are certain it was.

Exactly what is Nessie? There are several theories.

Bob Love believes that Nessie probably is a very large eel. Eels can fold up, which could account for the sightings of camellike humps. Eels lay eggs that hatch out into three-inch larvae. But a six-foot-long larva has been found and is being shown in Copenhagen, Denmark. An eel growing from such a larva would be ninety feet long.

Another theory says Nessie is a plesiosaur, a large, fish-eating reptile. "Plesiosaurs were plentiful about 65 million years ago," says an explorer, Jack Ullrich. "So they should be as extinct as all the other dinosaurs.

"But," he adds, "a living fish from the same age was discovered in 1947."

And why hasn't anyone found Nessie yet? One reason is that science is not ready to accept the fact that she exists.

A second drawback is money. Because there was not enough money, Bob Love and the bureau have had to use imagination in place of dollars to make inexpensive underwater flash cameras and other equipment.

But the money problem may be ending. Two months after my visit, scientists from London University said they had seen a family of similar monsters in Loch Morar, the deepest loch in Britain. Shortly after the Morar sightings, the Loch Ness Investigation Bureau received more money and will now be searching with better equipment.

Nessie herself may help in solving the mystery. A new power plant at the village of Foyers has forced Nessie to leave her favorite spot in the loch. She now comes to Urquhart Bay, where she has been surfacing more often than ever.

So chances of solving the centuries-old mystery are better than ever. All who have taken part in the search know there is something in Loch Ness. We would love to be there when that something is finally found. Wouldn't you?

MAKING YOUR OWN MONSTER

Make a papier-mâché miniature of one of the monsters you have read about, or make a monster of your own by following the directions below.

These are the things you will need:
  newspapers, flour, water, scissors, string, tempera paints, paintbrush, and bowl for mixing

This is what you will do:

Roll newspapers to form shapes for the body of the figure.

Wrap string tightly around the shapes to hold them together.

Cut newspapers into one-inch-wide strips. Mix flour and water to make a runny paste.

Dip paper strips into paste. Remove any extra paste by pulling the strips between your fingers. Wrap the strips around the rolled figure, keeping the strips as smooth as possible. When the entire figure is covered with two or three layers of strips, let it dry for at least 24 hours. Then cover the figure with two or more layers of pasted strips. Let dry.

To add shapes for features, use buttons, pipe cleaners, pieces of foam rubber or newspaper. Apply these shapes by using more glue or pasted strips.

Let the paste dry again for at least 24 hours. Then paint the figure with tempera paint. For a shiny finish, add one coat of shellac after the paint has dried.

The Gloom and the Din

In a setting of caverns and niches,
Lives a gaggle of wizards and witches
Who, with creatures of scale, fur, and feather,
Endure the most horrible weather.

The wizards keep mum during blizzards
While the witches converse with green lizards.
The witches keep still in typhoons
While the wizards commune with baboons.

Other beasts thus exposed to the gloom and the din
Did express their distress to the demon, a jinn.
He listened and then did loudly declare,
"This clamor must cease! It just isn't fair!"

So now though the weather's still dreary,
There can be heard a silence most eerie.
Thus if someone gets under your skin,
Send a call to your neighborhood jinn.

Shirley N. Austin

Ghost of the Lagoon

by Armstrong Sperry

The island of Bora Bora, where Mako lived, is far away in the South Pacific. It is not a large island—you can paddle around it in a single day. But the main body of Bora Bora rises straight out of the sea, very high into the air like a castle. Waterfalls tumble down the faces of the cliffs. As you look upward, you see wild goats leaping from rock to rock.

Mako had been born on the very edge of the sea. Most of his waking hours were spent in the waters of the lagoon, which was nearly enclosed by the two outstretched arms of the island. He was very clever with his hands.

He had made a spear that was as straight as an arrow and tipped with five iron points. He had made a canoe, hollowing it out of a tree. It wasn't a very big canoe—about five feet long. It had an outrigger, a sort of balance pole, fastened to one side to keep the boat from tipping over. The canoe was just large enough to hold Mako and his little dog Afa. They were great friends.

One evening Mako lay stretched at full length on the mats, listening to Grandfather's voice. Overhead, stars shone in the dark sky. From far off came the thunder of the surf on the reef.

The old man was speaking of Tupa, the ghost of the lagoon. Ever since the boy could remember, he had heard tales of this terrible monster. Frightened fishermen, returning from the reef at midnight, spoke of the ghost. Over the evening fires, old men told endless tales about the monster.

Not many people had ever seen the ghost of the lagoon. Grandfather was one of the few who had.

"What does it really look like, Grandfather?" the boy asked.

The old man shook his head slowly. The light from the cookfire shone on his white hair. "Tupa lives in the great caves of the reef. It is longer than this house. There is a sail on its back, not large, but terrible to see, for it burns with a white fire. Once when I was fishing beyond the reef at night, I saw it come up right under another canoe . . ."

"What happened then?" Mako asked. He half rose on one elbow. This was a story he had not heard before.

The old man's voice dropped to a whisper. "Tupa dragged the canoe right under the water—and the water boiled with white flame. The three fishermen in it were never seen

46

again. Fine swimmers they were, too."

Grandfather shook his head. "It is bad fortune even to speak of Tupa. There is evil in its very name."

"But King Opu Nui has offered a reward for its capture," the boy pointed out.

"Thirty acres of fine coconut land and a sailing canoe as well," said the old man. "But who ever heard of laying hands on a ghost?"

Mako's eyes glowed. "Thirty acres of land and a sailing canoe. How I should love to win that reward!"

Grandfather nodded, but Mako's mother scolded her son for such foolish talk. "Be quiet now, son, and go to sleep. Grandfather has told you that it is bad fortune to speak of Tupa. How well we have learned that lesson! Your father . . ." She stopped herself.

"What of my father?" the boy asked quickly. And now he sat up straight on the mats.

"Tell him, Grandfather," his mother whispered.

The old man cleared his throat and poked at the fire. A little shower of sparks whirled up into the darkness.

"Your father," he explained gently, "was one of the fishermen in the canoe that Tupa destroyed." His words fell upon the air like stones dropped into a deep well.

Mako shivered. He brushed back the hair from his damp forehead. Then he squared his shoulders and cried out fiercely, "I shall slay Tupa and win the King's reward!" He rose to his knees, his slim body tense, his eyes flashing in the firelight.

"Hush!" his mother said. "Go to sleep now. Enough of such foolish talk. Would you bring trouble upon us all?"

Mako lay down again upon the mats. He rolled over and closed his eyes, but sleep was long in coming.

The palm trees whispered above the dark lagoon, and far out on the reef the sea thundered.

The boy was slow to wake up the next morning. The ghost of Tupa had played through his dreams, making him restless. And so it was almost noon before Mako sat up on the mats and stretched himself. He called Afa, and the boy and his dog ran down to the lagoon for their morning swim.

When they returned to the house, wide awake and hungry, Mako's mother had food ready and waiting.

"These are the last of our bananas," she told him. "I wish you would paddle out to the reef this afternoon and bring back a new bunch."

The boy agreed eagerly. Nothing pleased him more than such an errand, which would take him to a little island on the outer reef half-a-mile from shore. It was one of Mako's favorite playgrounds, and there bananas and oranges grew in great plenty.

"Come, Afa," he called. "We're going on a journey." He picked up his long knife and grabbed his spear. A minute later he dashed across the white sand to where his canoe was tied up beyond the water's reach.

Afa barked wildly. He was all white except for a dark spot over each eye. Wherever Mako went, there went Afa also. Now the little dog leaped into the bow of the canoe, his tail wagging with delight. The boy shoved the canoe into the water and climbed aboard. Then picking up his paddle, he thrust it into the water. The sharp bow of the canoe cut through the green water of the lagoon like a knife through cheese. And so clear was the water that Mako could see the coral gardens, forty feet below him, growing in the sand. The shadow of the canoe moved over them.

A school of fish swept by like silver arrows. The boy thought suddenly of Tupa, ghost of the lagoon. On such a bright day it was hard to believe in ghosts of any sort. The fierce sunlight drove away all thought of them. Perhaps ghosts were only old men's stories, anyway!

Mako's eyes came to rest upon his spear—the spear that he had made with his own hands—the spear that was as straight and true as an arrow. He remembered his promise of the night before. Could a ghost be killed with a spear? Some night when all the village was sleeping, Mako thought to himself, he would find out! He would paddle out to the reef and challenge Tupa! Perhaps to-night. Why not? He caught his breath at the thought. A shiver ran down his back. His hands were tense on the paddle.

As the canoe drew away from shore, the boy saw the coral reef that above all others had always interested him. It was of white coral—a long, slim shape that rose slightly above the surface of the water. It looked very much like a shark. There was a ridge on the back that the boy could pretend was a dorsal fin, while up near one end were two dark holes that looked like eyes!

Times without number the boy had practiced spearing this make-believe shark, aiming always for the eyes, the most vulnerable spot. So true and straight had his aim become that the spear would pass right into the eyeholes without even touching the sides of the coral. Mako had named the coral reef "Tupa."

This morning, as he paddled past it, he shook his fist and called, "Tupa! Just wait till I get my bananas. When I come back, I'll make short work of you!"

Afa followed his master's words with a sharp bark. He knew Mako was excited about something.

The bow of the canoe touched the sand of the little island where the bananas grew. Afa leaped ashore and ran barking into the jungle.

Mako climbed into the shallow water, waded ashore, and pulled his canoe up on the beach. Then, picking up his banana knife, he followed Afa.

In the jungle the light was so dense and green that the boy felt as if he were moving underwater. Plants grew higher than his head. The branches of the trees formed a green roof over him.

Then, ahead of him, the boy saw the broad green blades of a banana tree. A bunch of bananas, golden ripe, was growing out of the top.

At the foot of the tree, Mako made a nest of soft leaves for the bunch to fall upon. In this way the fruit wouldn't be bruised. Then, with a swift slash of his blade, he cut the stem. The bananas fell to the earth. He found two more bunches.

Then he thought, "I might as well get some oranges while I'm here. The little oranges here are sweeter than any that grow on Bora Bora."

So he set about making a net of palm leaves in which to carry the oranges. As he worked, his swift fingers moving in and out among the strong green leaves, he could hear Afa's excited barks off in the jungle. That was just like Afa, always barking at something—a bird, a fish, a wild pig. He never caught anything either. Still, no boy ever had a finer animal friend.

The palm net took longer to make than Mako had realized. By the time it was finished and filled with oranges, the jungle was dark and gloomy. Night comes quickly and without warning in the islands of the tropics.

Mako carried the fruit down to the shore and loaded it into the canoe. Then he whistled to Afa. The dog came running out of the bush, wagging his tail.

"Hurry!" Mako scolded. "We won't be home before the dark comes."

The little dog leaped into the bow of the canoe, and Mako came aboard. Night seemed to rise up from the surface of the water and swallow them. On the far shore of Bora Bora, cookfires were being lighted. The first star twinkled just over the dark mountains. Mako dug his paddle into the water, and the canoe leaped ahead.

The dark water was alive with phosphorus. The bow of the canoe seemed to cut through a pale liquid fire. Each dip of the paddle left streamers of light. As the canoe approached the coral reef, the boy called, "Ho, Tupa! It's too late tonight to teach you your lesson. But I'll come back tomorrow." The coral shark glistened in the darkness.

And then suddenly Mako's breath caught in his throat. His hands felt weak. Just beyond the fin of the coral Tupa there was another fin—a huge one. It had never been there before. And—could he believe his eyes? It was moving.

The boy stopped paddling. He dashed his hand across his eyes. Afa began to bark. The great white fin, shaped like a small sail, glowed with phosphorescent light. Then Mako knew. Here was Tupa—the real Tupa—ghost of the lagoon!

Mako's knees felt weak. He tried to cry out, but his voice died in his throat. The great shark was circling slowly around the canoe. With each circle, it moved closer and closer. Now the boy could see the phosphorescent glow of the great shark's sides. As it moved in closer, he saw the yellow eyes and the gill slits in its throat.

Afa leaped from one side of the canoe to the other. In sudden anger, Mako leaned forward to grab the dog and

shake him soundly. Afa wriggled away as Mako tried to catch him, and the shift in weight tipped the canoe on one side. The outrigger rose from the water. In another second they would be overboard. The boy threw his weight over quickly to balance the canoe, but with a loud splash Afa fell over into the dark water.

Mako stared after him. The little dog, instead of swimming back to the canoe, had headed for the far shore. And there was the great white shark—very near.

"Afa! Afa! Come back! Come quickly!" Mako shouted.

The little dog turned back toward the canoe. He was swimming with all his strength. Mako leaned forward. Could Afa make it? Swiftly the boy grabbed his spear. Bracing himself, he stood upright. There was no weakness in him now. His dog, his friend, was in danger of instant death.

Afa was swimming desperately to reach the canoe. The white shark had paused in its circling to gather speed for the attack. Mako raised his arm, took aim. In that instant, the shark charged. Mako's arm flashed forward. All his strength was behind that thrust. The spear drove straight and true, right into the great shark's eye. Mad with pain and rage, Tupa whipped about in the water. The canoe rocked back and forth. Mako struggled to keep his balance as he drew back the spear by the cord fastened to his wrist.

He bent over to grab Afa and drag him aboard. Then he stood up, not a moment too soon. Once again the shark charged. Once again Mako threw his spear, this time at the other eye. The spear found its mark. Blinded and weak from loss of blood, Tupa rolled to the surface, turned slightly on its side. Was it dead?

Mako knew how clever sharks could be, and he was taking no chances. Hardly daring to breathe, he paddled toward the still body. He saw the great tail move slightly. The shark was still alive. The boy knew that one flip of that tail could overturn the canoe and send him and Afa into the water where Tupa could destroy them.

Swiftly, yet calmly, Mako stood upright and braced himself firmly. Then he threw his spear for the last time. Downward, swift as sound, the spear plunged into a white shoulder.

Peering over the side of the canoe, Mako could see the great fish turn over far below the surface. Then slowly, slowly, the great shark rose to the surface of the lagoon. There it floated.

Tupa was dead.

Mako flung back his head and shouted for joy. Hitching a strong line about the shark's tail, the boy began to paddle toward the shore of Bora Bora. The dorsal fin,

burning with the white fire of phosphorus, trailed after the canoe.

Men were running down the beaches of Bora Bora, shouting as they leaped into their canoes and put out across the lagoon. Their cries reached the boy's ears across the water.

"It is Tupa—ghost of the lagoon," he heard them shout. "Mako has killed it!"

That night, as the tired boy lay on the mats, listening to the distant thunder of the sea, he heard Grandfather singing a new song. It was the song that would be sung the next day at the feast that King Opu Nui would give in Mako's honor. The boy saw his mother bending over the cookfire. The stars leaned close, winking like friendly eyes. Grandfather's voice reached him now from a great distance, "Thirty acres of land and a sailing canoe . . ."

Living Pictures

Choose one of the pictures that you like in the story "Ghost of the Lagoon." Then think of yourself being in the picture. Express the sights, sounds, tastes, smells, and feelings you experience. Read the story again for other things to describe. Make a chart to show what you might have found while living in the picture.

For example, if you chose to be Mako in the picture on pages 44 and 45, you might have these experiences:

sights	mountains rising straight out of the sea
	goats leaping from rock to rock
sounds	waterfalls tumbling down the cliff
	surf thundering on the rocks
smells	fish frying for supper
	sweet scent of orange blossoms
tastes	sweet, juicy oranges
	cool coconut milk
feelings	proud of the spear
	happy as a bird singing in a tree

Listed below are some suggestions for things to do with the information you charted.

- Write a story or a song to express yourself.
- Create a special kind of poem. Word cinquains are fun to write. They are poems that have five lines and are put together this way:

Line 1: One word to give the title
Line 2: Two words to describe the title
Line 3: Three words to express action concerning the title
Line 4: Four words to express your feelings about the title
Line 5: Another word for the title

For example:

Land
Rich, rolling
Coconuts falling softly
Lovely flowers, ocean fun
Home

Picture yourself in a favorite or special place where you have been. Make a chart of your experiences. Use your imagination and have fun.

Books for You

The Greatest Monsters in the World by Daniel Cohen

This book explores the histories of monsters that some people believe may exist in the world today, such as sea monsters, Bigfoot, and others. Read the stories and draw your own conclusions as to whether these monsters do or do not exist.

The Monster Riddle Book by Jane Sarnoff and Reynold Ruffins

Laugh at the monsters by reading riddles about vampires, werewolves, ghosts, mummies, and other creatures.

Peter's Angel by Hope Campbell

Peter and his friends belong to a Monster Club and collect pictures and posters of all kinds of monsters. One day, some of the monsters decide to become real, and Peter creates an angel in hopes of counteracting them.

Sea Monsters by James B. Sweeney

Many eyewitness reports of sea monsters that have been sighted from 700 B.C. through the 1970's are recorded in this book.

Bigfoot All Over the Country by Marion T. Place

Did anyone ever report seeing a monster in your state? In this book you will read some fascinating stories about monsters that were sighted throughout most of the United States.

Europe On Wheels

"Always room for one more." My teacher talked almost to herself as she squeezed her motorcycle in between two parked cars on the school parking lot. She sures loves that bike!

"Have you ever taken a long trip on your motorcycle?" I asked.

"It's a real coincidence that you should ask that question, Tommy," she said. "Actually, no, I haven't taken a long trip on this bike. But my husband and I are going to travel through Europe this summer by motorcycle, camping along the way. We plan to buy a German touring bike in Munich and begin our trip from there. Now that my secret is out, maybe you and the rest of the class could help me plan the trip."

"Sure," I said. But what I was really thinking was, "Big deal! It sounds like work to me."

But once we got started, it was really fun. First thing we had to do was to help decide what to pack.

"Put out half of what you think is needed," our teacher said. "Then put half of that back."

Here is what we came up with for a two-month trip.

    1 tent
    2 sleeping bags
    1 rain suit each
    1 pair of shoes each
    2 helmets with face shields
    2 changes of clothes each
    soap, shampoo, detergent, towel,
        washcloth, comb
    first-aid kit

The next step was to "map out" the trip.

"My husband and I will be in Europe for fifty days. Some days we will not travel at all. And the most number of miles we would even consider traveling in one day would be 250 miles," my teacher told us. "Using these facts and a map of western Europe should give you an idea of how many cities we will be able to visit."

After choosing a route of countries, cities, and towns, we got together in small groups. Then we tried to find as much information as we could about the interesting places to visit in and around the different cities and towns.

By June all the plans were finished, and we were almost as excited about the trip as my teacher and her husband.

Western Europe

NORWAY

Oslo

SWEDEN

Stockholm

Baltic Sea

SCOTLAND

Glasgow

North Sea

DENMARK

Copenhagen

NETHERLANDS

IRELAND

Dublin

ENGLAND

London

BELGIUM

Amsterdam

Brussels

Berlin

EAST GERMANY

POLAND

Warsaw

Atlantic Ocean

Paris

Versailles

LUXEMBOURG

WEST GERMANY

Munich

Prague

CZECHOSLOVAKIA

Vienna

AUSTRIA

Budapest

HUNGARY

FRANCE

Bern

SWITZERLAND

ALPS

YUGOSLAVIA

Belgrade

Adriatic Sea

Marseilles

Florence

Rome

ITALY

PYRENEES

CORSICA

Lisbon

PORTUGAL

Madrid

Tossa

SPAIN

MALLORCA

SARDINIA

SICILY

ALBANIA

Mediterranean Sea

AFRICA

Then summer vacation came and went, and I almost forgot about my teacher and her motorcycle. But on that first morning back at school, there she was again in the school parking lot.

"Always room for one more," she said almost to herself as she squeezed her beautiful new touring motorcycle in between two cars.

"Wow!" I said. "That sure is a neat bike."

She patted it. "That's not just a bike, Tommy. That's a beautiful machine," she told me. "Want to hear more about it?"

What could I say but, "Sure"? "The other kids will want to hear, too," I went on. "Going to tell us about Europe?"

She laughed. "I thought you'd never ask," she said.

The Trip

"Seeing so many places that we had heard and studied about was quite an experience by itself. But seeing everything from the motorcycle made the trip even more special.

"The only disadvantages we could foresee were laundry and the weather. We washed our clothes by hand every

night because we only had two changes of clothes. They were always dry the next day. As for the rain, it was fun getting wet. We had rain suits that usually kept our clothes dry. There were only a few times when we were very wet and chilled. Those nights we stayed in a guest house or a hotel so we wouldn't get sick.

"Unless other people have experienced motorcycling, it is difficult to explain its thrills and excitement without sounding corny. But there were many advantages to camping and motorcycling—50 miles to a gallon of gas, spending only a few dollars to camp, always finding a place to park, experiencing everything with all five senses, a friendly wave from a passing biker, always finding someone to talk to or trade stories with.

"We took almost four hundred pictures in the two months that we were gone. We also kept a daily notebook describing the places we visited, the people we met, and some funny things that happened to us along the way. Because of the pictures and the notebook, we will always be able to remember what a great time we had that summer. And we were able to share it with our relatives, our friends, and especially our students. What a thrill it was for us, and I hope it has been thrilling for you to see the results of your effort, your planning, your enthusiasm, and your ideas. I'll leave the notebook in the classroom library. You are welcome to look through it whenever you wish."

"She's really something," I said to no one in particular as I strolled to my desk. Wouldn't you know it—she heard me, winked, and said, "Next trip we'll see if we can find room for you. There's always room for one more."

Munich, Germany. Jerry is packing some gear after our first night of camping.

We met two guys from Sweden and two girls from London at the campground in Versailles, France. We went into Paris with them and had a great time.

The campground in Marseilles, France, was right on a beach of the Mediterranean.

We took a four-day "vacation" from our trip and just relaxed in Tossa, Spain.

As we were rounding a curve in the Alps, we nearly collided with this French-woman's goat herd.

Here I am enjoying one of the many open-air markets in Florence, Italy.

♦ And the Winner Is!

Congratulations! You and a friend have just won an exciting, expense-paid, three-week motorcycle tour of the state or country of your choice!

Decide where you wish to go and find it on a map. Choose the route you wish to take.

Make a scrapbook or a daily journal of the places you want to visit each day and include a picture or a brief description of each. (Sources of information about points of interest include the library card catalog, encyclopedias, travel bureaus, chambers of commerce of U.S. cities, and embassies of foreign countries.)

After you have completed your plans for this fantastic trip, you will probably be an expert on the area you plan to visit. But share your plans and your journal with your classmates. They may just have some helpful comments or good suggestions.

CYCLE CARTOONS

The Touring Biker's Highway

Somewhere there's a great smooth highway
With sloping turns and gentle bends
That leads from here and now
And never really ends.

It runs through soft green meadows
Beside shimmering mountain lakes
With a variety of scenery
Around each bend it takes.

There are many quiet forests
The silver threaded streams
Running through the kind of land
Usually found in dreams.

I have never really found it
Though I've come close a time or two
So I'll just travel down each highway
Until someday I do.

I'll feel the winds that greet me
And catch a whiff of fragrant scent
From the forest along that highway
And wonder where it went.

Maybe around another turn
I'll see that mountain lake
Or I'll find that big broad highway
Down each road I take.

So I roll the throttle over
And hear the engine roar
And head towards the setting sun
To try again, once more.

Don Smith

 SLIDEOUT

by John P. Covington

The two motorcycles sped easily between the steel posts
that had been planted to stop cars and rumbled over a
narrow wooden bridge.

Leodus Jackson, the first rider to cross, waved his hand
toward a grassy hill. Engines snarled as the riders geared
down for the climb. Rising to a crouch on their footpegs,
they raced up the hill over the grass. At the top, they
pulled the bikes to a standstill and looked back.

Eddie Moats reached out a gloved hand to switch off
his engine.

"Nobody here," he shouted above the sound of the other machine.

Leodus thumbed the kill-button on his handlebars, and in the sudden quiet both riders took off their helmets and looked out over the green Connecticut countryside.

A little village of white wooden houses stood in the valley to their left, but mostly the riders were surrounded by woodland. They could see a ribbon of asphalt in the valley floor, twisting up around the hill on which they sat.

"That must be the track," Eddie said. "Look, it goes under the bridge."

"Yeah, and here comes trouble," Leodus said. A car pulling a trailer appeared suddenly on the bridge. "Wonder how he got here."

They watched the car suspiciously, but it turned onto a side road that led toward the track, not paying any attention to them. The trailer carried a little racing car that looked like a ballpoint pen with four fat tires. Before long, other cars were rumbling over the bridge and heading down the side road.

"I guess we're going to see some action," Eddie said. "The newspaper said that four cars crashed in a single accident last week. Nobody was hurt, but think how much those cars cost!"

"Who cares? I'd like to get me one of those." Leodus pointed to a large, wedge-shaped racer with an odd-looking airplane flap sticking up on poles off the back.

"Sure, Lee. What are you going to do, drive it down 125th Street? That car will do two hundred miles an hour."

A little green truck rumbled across the bridge. Its driver waved to them. They waved back as the truck disappeared down the side road. Soon they heard the scream of unmuffled engines from somewhere below the hill.

The little racer appeared on the track, moving very slowly at first. Its engine note rose and fell as the driver fed it gas and then backed off. Once he was sure that the engine was warm, he eased out the clutch fully and accelerated forward

through a group of turns called "the esses" after the shape of the letter S. The boys heard its tires howling and its engine sound rise with each gear change until it disappeared into the narrow cut that passed under the bridge.

Other cars appeared on the track, different sizes and styles for different racing classes. This was Tuesday, the day the track was open for practice sessions. Eddie and Lee had agreed to take the day off and ride up for a look.

Eddie Moats was known for being a scrapper. He was small and quick, a fast talker. His hair was wavy black, and his eyes were gray with a fierce glow.

Restless, in a hurry to try out anything new, Eddie managed to rub most people the wrong way. And he was as hardheaded as he was quick. He found himself in more fights than he started. Not that he minded. He'd grown up in the streets of Hoboken, on the New Jersey waterfront, where he had learned about self-defense early in life.

The job from which he and Lee had taken the day off was the only one Eddie had held for more than a few weeks. He worked at the studio of Paul Caesar, a New York photographer. Eddie had stayed on for the better part of a year now, probably because something new was always happening.

Eddie, at nineteen, had been put in charge of the lights and backgrounds for the picture sessions. He handled some of the cameras as well. Lee helped with the camera and worked in the darkroom on processing the film.

They were the same age, but they couldn't exactly be called a matched pair. Lee was taller, slower-moving. He made plans, and he was careful. He wanted to get out of Harlem, and photography looked like a good route. And Paul Caesar was one of the best photographers in the business. On the whole Lee seemed older than Eddie, but in spite of their different styles, the two didn't get in each other's way. In fact, they had become close friends.

Now the wedge-shaped racer was in sight again, thrusting into the turn. It had been gaining speed each lap. Attempting a four-wheel slide called a "drift," the driver overcompensated. Instead of sliding sideways to the edge of the pavement, then accelerating forward in a new direction, the car continued off onto slippery grass and did two quick spins.

"Wow!" Lee said. "He didn't hit anything! He didn't even turn over!"

The driver took off his helmet to check the car but didn't even get out of the cockpit. Glancing up at the hill, he saw the boys and grinned. Then he turned the car around and pulled to the edge of the track. Before he could return to the pavement he had to wait for an even smaller vehicle. With a fierce scream of exhaust, a yellow motorcycle roared into the turn and slashed its way up through the esses.

"Did you see that?" Eddie jumped to his feet. "A bike out on the track!"

"And he was really moving."

"Lee, what do you say? Should we have a go at it?"

"Are you crazy? Man, if you get anywhere near that track, they'll throw you in a country jail forever. You know what they think about bikes out here."

Eddie hurried toward his motorcycle and folded out the kick starter. "Maybe they don't think what we think they think. Take a look." He nodded toward the track, throwing the weight of his wiry body into the kick. Out on the track a cluster of four bikes shot by in tight formation. Eddie's engine started with a roar.

"Coming?"

Lee went slowly over to his bike. He swung his leg over the big Harley and with two thrusts of the kick starter brought the engine to life.

Following wooden arrows bearing the word "Pits," they took the side road to a large, open parking lot. Racing cars and other vehicles were scattered about the lot, surrounded by mechanics and drivers. Open toolboxes, cans of gas and oil, tires and tire-changing equipment stood near the waiting machines.

Most of the bikes were grouped near the far end of the lot. As the boys moved in that direction, a man carrying a clipboard removed himself from a cluster around one of the cars and started toward them on foot. The two riders stopped their machines and glanced at each other.

"You fellows want to use the track?" the man asked.

"Sure," Eddie said, trying to sound casual. "What do we have to do?"

The man seemed friendly enough, but he didn't answer at once. His eyes studied the machines quickly and expertly. Eddie was glad both bikes were in top shape. Every nut and bolt was tight, every wire and cable taped neatly in place. The bikes were also clean, carefully wiped free of road dirt. The man's attention shifted to their riding equipment: leather jackets, boots, gloves, helmets.

"It'll cost you five dollars a bike," he said at last. "You sign this paper, and you go on the track when the starter sends you out. There are enough bikes here now to run separately from the cars. Twenty minutes on, twenty minutes off. Tape your headlights and wire up your stands."

Eddie glanced over at Lee. Five bucks was five bucks, but they couldn't expect it to be free. He took out his money and counted seven dollars. "OK," he said, handing five to the man.

"Maybe next time," Lee said, as if to suggest that he was short of money. Eddie guessed there was another reason. Lee probably doubted that a racetrack was right for his big Harley. Faster and more powerful than Eddie's Triumph, it might not handle well on the twisting course.

Eddie signed the paper on the clipboard. It contained a lot of legal language meaning he was on his own. If anyone got hurt, he couldn't hold the track responsible or expect anybody to pay doctor bills.

"Keep your eye on the starter," the man said. "Yellow flag means one more lap. Black flag means stop and return to the pits immediately. Red flag means danger."

"By the way," he added, "you should have full leathers. The rules require them on race day. I think Hans—over there with the green truck—has an extra set. You might ask to borrow them."

Eddie nodded as they restarted their machines. Threading through the pits, they found an empty spot next to the green truck. Behind it stood the yellow bike they had seen on the track. A rider their age was fixing its rear chain. He looked up as they stopped and dismounted.

"Bike session starts in about ten minutes," he said. "You guys going out on the track?"

"I am," Eddie said. He was feeling uneasy. He was a good street rider, but he had never been on a racetrack before. It would be easy to make a fool of himself or to give it too much and throw away his bike.

The guy reached into his toolbox, picked out a roll of tape, and tossed it to Eddie. "Here, better tape up that headlight."

"Thanks," Eddie said. He had no idea where to put the tape but began applying strips anyway.

The other rider laughed. "No, man, the lens! A crisscross pattern on the lens. They don't want glass all over the track if you spill."

Eddie winced and started taping the lens. The other rider got up and came over, grinning.

"My name is Hans Brendhal," he said, holding out a hand.

"Eddie Moats," said Eddie. "This is Lee."

"Lee Jackson," Lee said, shaking hands.

Hans nodded to Eddie. "You haven't got time to get that junk off, but you'd better wire up those stands. Have you got the oil tank and plug safely wired?"

"No," Eddie said, objecting to the word *junk.* "We weren't told anything about that."

"They will on race day. Nobody wants to go sliding around in your oil when those plugs shake out. Anyway, make sure they're tight."

Eddie got out his bike's tiny tool kit and checked the plugs. They were all tight. He took the length of wire that he carried in the kit and cut it in half. While Lee held the bike, he wired the sidestand and centerstand to the frame so they couldn't swing down.

"All set."

"Except for the leathers," Hans said. "I don't figure Stan sent you over here for nothing." He reached in the truck and pulled out a bundle of black leather. "This old suit has been used a lot, but it's still good." Eddie muttered thanks, unfolding the leather bundle. It was a one-piece leather suit with a zipper down the front.

As Hans pushed his bike off toward the track, Eddie quickly put on the leather suit. The leather was stiff and dirty, and he noticed that the suit had been patched often. He put on his boots and helmet.

"Here goes nothing," Eddie told Lee as he took the bike and began pushing toward the group of riders waiting by the track.

"Good luck, man," Lee said, his look of concern saying everything he wasn't.

Overhead, a loudspeaker crackled. "OK, motorcycles on the track for twenty minutes. Don't go wide on turn one, there's new pavement. Watch the flagman." The speaker crackled again, then clicked off.

Most of the riders started their engines immediately and swarmed onto the track.

Eddie fired up and rode to the track's edge. Only one rider remained in sight—down by the first turn where his engine must have died. Eddie's heart set a pounding rhythm. "Let's go," he told himself. He rolled on the throttle and eased out the clutch.

The Triumph leaped forward, and Eddie was in the center of the main straightaway, headed for turn one, a righthander that led into the esses. He changed up to second gear when the tachometer reached 6,000 rpm, and to third when the tach again read 6,000 rpm. He knew the straightaway was the fastest part of the course, but he didn't have enough distance to get into fourth gear before slowing down for the turn. The black asphalt pavement was slightly rippled from the pounding of big race cars. Counting mostly on engine braking, he just touched his brakes lightly before leaning the bike over into the turn.

It was a good feeling, having the whole roadway to himself with no worries that anyone might be coming the other way. He could choose his own "line" through the turns, swinging from one side of the pavement to the other along the fastest path. Eddie leaned sharply to the left and then again to the right as the course changed

direction. He got through the esses and started up the hill at the back of the course.

It was there that the first motorcycle passed him. Hans Brendhal on his yellow racer shot by on the inside of the turn. Eddie watched as its front wheel lifted slightly, responding as Hans accelerated over the top of the hill. Eddie followed, heading slightly downhill into the cut under the bridge and then more steeply onto a short downhill straight. A right-hander led back onto the main straight. It was a dangerous turn. Eddie emerged on the main straight at about 40 mph, just in time to see Hans dive into turn one—over a quarter of a mile away.

"So much for the slow lap, now for some speed." Eddie wound the engine up to 7,200 rpm before shifting into third and watched the tach needle drop back to 5,000. It climbed again to 7,200: 85 mph. He shifted to fourth. He crouched low on the bike to cut down wind resistance, his chest on the gas tank, his elbows in close. The tach needle was climbing more slowly now. As it hit 6,200, three bikes passed him on the right. He knew they were going well over 100 mph.

All four riders sat up at once. The blast of wind hit Eddie hard on the face and chest, his body acting as a kind of sail to help the motorcycle slow down for turn one. Eddie applied the brakes as hard as he could, felt the bike shudder and hop as it lost speed. Still, it passed the other three bikes, much lighter racing machines with racing brakes. Then Eddie realized that he was going too fast to make the turn. There was an oily shine to the pavement on the outside of the turn. Just a little too fast, he thought, but he didn't want to drop his motorcycle.

He continued off the end of the straight onto a narrow escape road. The bike rolled to a stop, and Eddie just sat there for a minute, shaking a little from excitement. The leathers, no longer stiff, were now wet with sweat. He put the bike back into gear and returned to the track. Trying to hide his embarrassment, he pretended not to notice Lee waving to him from the pit entrance.

Eddie took the next few laps carefully, adding a little speed each time. As he grew more familiar with the turns, he learned to avoid the rough patches and the slippery spots. The bike was running well. His Triumph had almost as much acceleration as the racers but couldn't match them in top speed or braking.

Eddie was having a ball, doing what he liked best. In turn one, the bike heeled over so far that the edge of his boot touched the pavement. A yellow blur suddenly appeared beside him. Hans, cornering hard, passed him on the outside. Eddie couldn't resist. He twisted a little more throttle and leaned his Triumph still deeper into the turn. The footpeg growled on the pavement. The yellow figure dropped from sight.

The next turn was a lefthander and, if Hans got beside him, the yellow bike would be on the inside for a better line. Eddie gave it all the throttle he could coming out of the righthander, straightened up, then heeled the bike hard to the left. Again he saw the yellow blur easing up beside him. He could almost touch the other machine with his elbow. But he was a wheel-and-a-half ahead and first into the turn. He could have crowded into the edge of the pavement, forcing the other machine over. Instead, he stayed out about a yard and held as much speed as he could.

The left footpeg was scraping the pavement now, quickly wearing through the rubber to the steel. Too much pressure on that peg would cause the rear wheel to leave the ground and drop the bike. Eddie held on. It was a long turn. A tiny oil spot or a patch of gravel would slide out a wheel, too, but Eddie remembered where they were and avoided them. He didn't dare glance back, but the yellow blur didn't reappear.

Eddie held his pace through the esses and on up the hill at the back of the course. His bike still wore its street mufflers, and he could hear the angry snarl of the racer behind him. He was taking chances, driving over his head. His hands and arms were aching with tension. Near the bottom of the downhill straight, he shot a quick glance behind. Hans was twenty yards away.

A righthander, and Eddie was out on the front straight. As he sped past the starting tower flat on the tank, the yellow racer went by, leading him into turn one.

"I'll catch him," Eddie told himself, driving hard into the turn.

By the end of the long lefthander, Eddie's front tire was right behind the yellow racer. As they accelerated toward the next righthander, he wound out his engine to 7,500 rpm, explosion level. He held on an instant longer when Hans braked for the turn, and the Triumph slipped by. Eddie got into the turn, but the bike was way over

and surging. Every surge drove the footpeg into the pavement. Too fast, he realized. The rear wheel let go, and he felt a sharp blow on his shoulder. Then everything was spinning end over end.

It was like slow motion. He couldn't stop himself; he just kept tumbling. The sun flashed off the bright blue Triumph as it tumbled ahead of him. He came to a stop, lying numb in the grass.

People were crowding around. "He was riding on street tires!" he heard an incredulous voice say.

Lee bent down to him. "Eddie! Hey, man, you all right?"

Eddie lifted himself up on one elbow and looked around. The Triumph lay in the grass, its headlight smashed. He looked at the people and then turned to Lee, grinning.

"Sure, never better."

Motorcycle Jargon

Every sport has its own language, or jargon. Do you know the jargon of motorcycling? Play this game with friends.

Get a large piece of cardboard, twenty small cards, a pencil, a ruler, paints or crayons, and one toy motorcycle or other marker for each player.

Do this:
- Copy the racetrack on the cardboard or design your own game board.
- Write the words below on the cards. Write one word on the front of each card.

gear	leather	throttle	kill-button
drift	clutch	flagman	accelerate
esses	cockpit	footpeg	handlebars
track	exhaust	slideout	tachometer
helmet	kick starter	straightaway	overcompensate

- Write the word's meaning on the back of the card. Check "Slideout" or a dictionary if you need help.

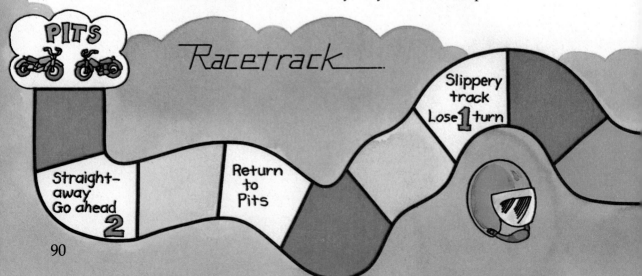

- Assign a number value from 1 (easy) to 5 (difficult) to each word.
- Write the number in the card's upper right corner.

front   back

Play the game.
- Place the markers in the *Pits.*
- Place the word cards face up in a pile.
- The player chooses the top card, reads the word, and tells its meaning. The player then turns the card over and reads the meaning.
- If correct, the player keeps the card and moves his or her marker the number of spaces shown on the card.
- If incorrect, the player returns the card face up to the pile.
- If a player lands on a space with a direction, he or she follows the direction.
- The first player to cross the finish line wins.

To make a new game, change the word cards. Use the jargon of your favorite sport.

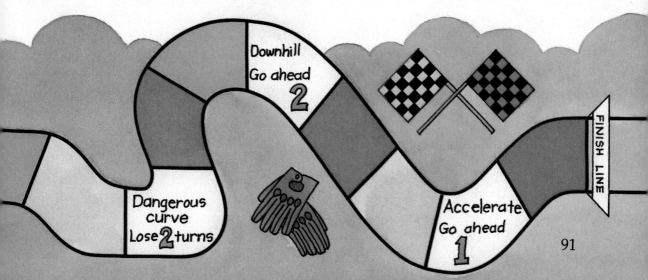

MOTORCYCLE RACES

by Nicole Puleo

Drag Racing

Of all the kinds of motorcycle racing, drag racing is one of the most exciting. The smell of burning rubber, the loud roar of the engines, the extremely high speeds—all these things are part of drag racing. Drag-racing tracks are perfectly straight. They are only a quarter of a mile long from start to finish. The object of drag racing is to travel from the starting line to the finish line in as little time as possible. Thus speed is king in drag racing.

Specially built drag motorcycles have covered the quarter-mile strip in less than ten seconds by reaching speeds of over 160 mph!

Time trials are used in motorcycle drag races to weed out some of the competing riders. Each bike must make at least one timed run down the track. Only the riders with the best times qualify for the races against other riders, instead of against the clock.

Motocross

Motocrosses, which are run on dirt tracks, are more physically demanding than any other type of motorcycle competition. They are also more popular. Between half a mile and a mile and a half long, the dirt tracks used for motocrosses are obstacle courses. These courses include jumps and bumps, mud and sand, hills and ruts, water crossings, and gullies. To win in motocross, a rider must be more than skilled; a rider must also be tough.

Most motocrosses consist of three short races, or "motos," which can last from as little as fifteen to as much as forty-five minutes each. Speed is what counts in a motocross. In each moto, the rider who completes the most laps in a given amount of time wins the most points. At the end of all three motos, the rider who has the most points is the winner. Even if a rider wins the first two motos, that rider can still lose the motocross by failing to compete or to do well in the final moto. This is why it is so important for a motocross rider to have enough strength and endurance to compete in all three motos.

Enduro

An enduro event is a motorcycle race that is not a test of speed. Rather, it is a test of rider and machine endurance in tough motorcycle competition. Enduro riders pace their riding to follow a time schedule. They are racing against the clock rather than against other racers.

Most enduro courses are from fifty to as much as two hundred and fifty miles long. The courses cover open meadows, mountain trails, paved and dirt roads, riverbanks, streams, swamps, and deserts. Since many enduro courses are designed like cloverleafs, certain sections of the courses are repeated by the riders several times.

About a week before an enduro event is scheduled, a crew marks out the course and sets up checkpoints for the race. These checkpoints are flag-marked places at which each rider must arrive during the course of the race. The object of the race is to get from one checkpoint to the next in the exact amount of time given in the time schedule. In order to arrive at each checkpoint on time, riders must keep a certain average speed. This means that they must slow down and speed up to keep that average speed when traveling from one checkpoint to the next.

Each rider is given a "route card" an hour before the race begins. The route card tells the riders the starting time, the locations of the checkpoints, and the distances between the checkpoints. The card also gives the average speeds needed to get from checkpoint to checkpoint in the amount of time allowed.

In most enduros, riders start the race at one-minute intervals. If the starting time of an enduro is 8:00 A.M., rider number one starts the race at 8:01, rider number two starts at 8:02, and so on, until every rider has begun

the race. In cases where there are hundreds of entries in an enduro, the riders sometimes start in groups of three.

Each rider in an enduro begins the event with a total of 1,000 points and tries to lose as few points as possible. The rider who loses the fewest points is the winner. Points can be lost at two kinds of checkpoints—"known" checkpoints, which are known to the rider before the race begins, and "secret" checkpoints, which the rider does not know about ahead of time. A rider loses one point for every minute late at a known or secret checkpoint. At secret checkpoints, there is a loss of two points for every minute early! In most one-day enduros, the winner of the race has lost fewer than ten points.

Louise Scherbyn: Pioneer Cyclist

by Alice Turner

Starting with her first shaky ride on a 1932-model Indian Pony motorcycle, Louise Scherbyn went on to become a pioneer in women's motorcycling.

Louise has owned three bikes, all Indians. Her first was the 1932 Pony. Her second was a 1936 Scout. She rode it

in the *First All-Girl Motorcycle Show* in the United States. The last machine she bought was a 1940 Indian Scout, which she bought new with a special paint job and white saddlebags. She still has the Scout and has no plans to replace it.

Through the years Louise has taken part in field meets, endurance runs, cross-country road races, and other motorcycle events.

Louise retired her Indian in 1960—but she hasn't retired from motorcycling. In 1950 she founded the Women's International Motorcycle Association. She is still its president and the editor of the club's newsletter. The club now has over 1,000 members worldwide and it is still growing.

Besides being active in the Women's International Motorcycle Association, Louise also finds time to collect miniature and toy motorcycles. Her collection of more than 350 pieces contains small cycles made of iron, tin, lead, brass, plaster, plastic, wood, glass, rubber, cardboard, cloth, and even silver. Most of these are toys, although some are in the form of charms, pins, and even useful items such as can openers and pencil sharpeners. Her collection contains military bikes from both World Wars, police bikes, service cycles, and pleasure bikes. There is a group of circus clowns, monkeys, and some cartoon characters riding motorcycles.

Louise started her collection in 1933. Each motorcycle is numbered and recorded in a special book that tells when and where it was bought or received. Many of them were bought during her travels, but she has received a lot of her collection as gifts from friends. This miniature cycling museum is located in the Scherbyn home in Waterloo, New York.

Describe-a-Person Puzzle

Louise Scherbyn was a pioneer in women's motorcycling. To be a pioneer, a person must have certain qualities, such as courage and perseverance, to reach a desired goal.

After reading "Louise Scherbyn: Pioneer Cyclist" and looking at the photographs, how would you describe Louise? What kind of a person do you think she is?

Now see if you can work this puzzle.
- Write the last name of the pioneer cyclist on your paper. Write the letters of her name in a column.
- For each letter in the name, think of a word that could describe Louise.
- On your paper, write the word beside the letter. The first one is done for you.

    S - strong
    c
    h
    e
    r
    b
    y
    n

If you need help, look for clues in the box below. Begin with an underlined letter and read across or down.

a	b	<u>b</u>	d	e	f	g	h	i	j	k	l
<u>c</u>	<u>r</u>	e	s	p	o	n	s	i	b	l	e
a	<u>e</u>	a	g	e	r	<u>h</u>	a	r	d	<u>y</u>	m
r	n	u	o	p	q	r	s	t	u	o	v
e	<u>s</u>	t	r	o	n	g	w	x	y	u	z
f	<u>n</u>	i	m	b	l	e	c	d	e	n	f
u	g	f	h	i	j	k	l	m	n	g	o
l	p	u	q	r	s	t	u	v	w	x	y
z	a	l	b	c	d	e	f	g	h	i	j

You may choose other words if they describe the cyclist.

Think of another famous person. Make a Describe-a-Person puzzle about that person. Let your friends work the puzzle. Be sure to supply some clues, too.

The Third Wheel

In the early 1900's a French Army sergeant invented a cart with one wheel and a seat. This invention, which was attached to the side of a motorcycle, became known as a sidecar.

Most people don't know much about sidecars, or they consider them a thing of the past. Actually, sidecars are becoming more popular among motorcyclists in this country. Meet two people whose business is sidecars—buying, restoring, and selling them.

Bill Heggarty and Brian Casey own a shop in St. Louis, Missouri, where they restore old sidecars. Their shop is in the garage of an old mansion. The boys and girls in the neighborhood come by to watch the restoring and sometimes even to do little errands.

The first step is to find old sidecars. Sidecars were once very popular in Europe. Most of them can be found there in some strange places like junkyards, farmers' barns, and old motor shops piled with junk. Once in a while some sidecars will be found in the same kinds of places in the United States. The sidecars found in Europe are shipped from Bremen, Germany, to Chicago, Illinois. Bill and Brian pick them up by truck and take them back to their shop.

It is then that the work of restoring the sidecars begins. The work takes about four weeks, and there are nine steps in the process.

1. Sandblast to remove rust and old paint.
2. Remove dents.
3. Send all metal parts to the plater.
4. Apply primer (3 coats).
5. Apply wet sand primer.
6. Apply color paint (2 coats).
7. Paint stripes.
8. Apply two coats of clear paint.
9. Assemble the car, re-spoke the wheels, and upholster.

People from all over the world order sidecars from Bill and Brian. One recently finished order was a beautiful white German Steib sidecar. Brian attached the car to the left side of the motorcycle instead of to the right side like some of the others in the shop. He explained that the customer who ordered this particular car lives in England, where people drive on the left side of the road. In our country, where we drive on the right side of the road, sidecars are attached to the right side. This is so that the driver can see when passing a car.

Restoring sidecars is a business with a limited future because the supply of old sidecars might soon run out. But by then, Bill and Brian hope that they will have a license to sell and service motorcycles.

Make Your Own Sidecar

If you could build your own sidecar, how would you want it to look? Put your ideas on paper first. Begin by designing the body style of the car. This is the most important part.

Once you have the body style, plan how you might decorate the car. Choose the paint color or colors and the material for the seat cover. Add extras such as a windshield, handle grips, pockets or shelves, and whatever else you'd like to have on your sidecar.

Here are some examples of customized sidecars.

When the drawing of your customized sidecar is finished, you might want to try making an actual model from the plans, using soap or an easily carved wood, like balsa.

Books for You

Gasoline Cowboy by William Campbell Gault

Rex Smalley loves motorcycles and dreams of being the number-one rider. This dream takes Rex, a "gasoline cowboy," from his home in Texas around the country. Finally he meets Hud Eggleton in a showdown for the championship.

A Complete Beginner's Guide to Motorcycling
by Bernhard A. Roth

This book answers questions about buying, licensing, riding, and using motorcycles. The author gives advice on motorcycle safety and protection for riders of all ages.

Motorcycle Motocross School by Ed and Dan Radlauer

Photos and detailed information about motorcycles and racing are presented by the authors.

The Mouse and the Motorcycle by Beverly Cleary

In this humorous fantasy, a mouse named Ralph makes friends with a boy named Keith. Keith's toy motorcycle happens to be just the right size for Ralph.

The Complete Motorcycle Book by Lyle Kenyon Engel

Here is a fascinating account of how motorcycles developed. There is advice on how to buy and to ride a cycle. The reader can also take a look at the future of two-wheeled vehicles.

The $tory of Money

edited by Klaus Heidensohn

Money has no real value of its own. It is only a token. Yet it is accepted by everyone, everywhere. It would be hard to imagine the world without money. But not all people throughout history have used it.

There is nothing mysterious about money. It is simply something that is commonly used for the buying and the selling of services and goods of trade. This is how the idea of money got started.

Trading

Long ago people traded what they didn't want for something they needed or wanted. Hunters who had more animal skins than they could use often traded for pretty beads to decorate the skins. No money changed hands.

Then came bartering.

Bartering

For many centuries bartering was the means of exchanging services and goods. Each person placed a value on his or her services and goods and exchanged them for other services or goods. Let's see what might happen if you had a tiger skin and needed corn.

How much corn could you get for one tiger skin if three bushels of corn were equal to five bananas, twenty bananas were equal to one goat, and twenty goats were equal to one tiger skin?

Then came tokens.

Tokens

It was very difficult and it took too much time to find someone who had what you wanted and who was willing to give you what you thought was a fair exchange. For this reason, tokens were invented. The token was something that was commonly accepted by the people and had a value agreed upon. What was used as a token depended upon the way of life in the community. For example, hunting communities often used skins. The people of Tibet used a brick of tea, and shell money was used in New Guinea.

Then came coins.

Coins

Tokens worked well within a community, but world trade demanded a medium of exchange that could be found in other lands. Such things as cowrie shells and bamboo pieces were useless as a worldwide means of exchange because they were not available in other countries.

According to stories, around 650 B.C. a king of Lydia had the idea of issuing what are now called coins. This

idea spread very rapidly. The coins provided a common means by which to value many different kinds of services and goods.

The idea of coins was good, but it had some problems. Think of how hard it would be to carry large bags of heavy metal coins from one place to another. It is not surprising, then, that someone had the idea of making paper money. Records show that as early as the ninth century B.C. the banks in China issued bank notes, or paper money. On the notes was printed "to be circulated as cash."

The Future of Money

At the moment, credit cards are a convenient way of buying goods and services. Will the use of credit cards be extended? Will there be a change to computer money that will cause coins and notes to disappear? The future of money will largely depend upon changes in society. Only time will tell.

Travel the Money Road

Imagine that you stepped into a time machine and found yourself back in the year 3000 B.C. What interesting changes in money would you see as you traveled the highway back to the present day?

To show what happened to money throughout the years, draw a highway on a large sheet of paper. Put in the milestones as shown below. Between each milestone, write the events in the order in which they happened during that period. You will find a list of events and the time each happened on the next page. The first one is done for you. Decorate your highway with pictures of some of the events you thought were most interesting.

3000 B.C. Sumerians began to use metal coins to replace barley.

3000 B.C.–
A.D. 500

A.D. 501–
A.D. 1000

A.D. 1001–
A.D. 1500

A.D. 1501–
A.D. 1600

A.D. 1601–
A.D. 1700

A.D. 1701–
A.D. 1800

A.D. 1801–
A.D. 1900

A.D. 1901–
A.D. 2000

A.D. 2001–
?

Some important money events.

3000 B.C.	Sumerians began to use metal coins to replace barley.
A.D. 1613	Copper coins came into use.
A.D. 1873	U.S. adopted the gold standard.
A.D. 615	"Burning oil" (petroleum) was used as money.
A.D. 1608	The first checks, called cash letters, were used in the Netherlands.
A.D. 1871	Germany adopted the gold standard.
A.D. 695	The first Arab coins were made.
700 B.C.	Coins in Lydia were made of a gold-silver metal.
A.D. 1252	Golden florins were minted in Florence, Italy.
A.D. 1661	The first gold guinea pieces were coined in England.
A.D. 1924	Bartering returned to Germany for a short time.
A.D. 1662	The last silver pennies were minted in London.
A.D. 1861	U.S. government issued paper money.
A.D. 1661	The first paper money in Europe was used in Stockholm.
A.D. 1923	The value of the German mark dropped until 4,000,000 equaled only one U.S. dollar.
A.D. 650	The earliest forms of paper money were issued in China.
A.D. 1681	The first checks were used in England.
A.D. 1787	Dollar currency was introduced in the U.S.
350 B.C.	The first Roman coins were made.
A.D. 1685	The first Canadian paper money was used.
A.D. 1873	Germany adopted the mark as a unit of currency.
A.D. 1970	Use of credit cards increased in the U.S.
A.D. 1718	The first bank notes were used in England.
A.D. 2000	What will it be?

Skiddley, Broadwaller, and the Pot of Gold

retold by Solveig Paulson Russell

Once there were two leprechauns walking in the woods on a fine March day. One was a young fellow who wore his feather-trimmed cap way back on his head. The feather flipped and danced in every breeze. The other wee person was an old-time, dyed-in-the-green leprechaun who had lived through many Irish summers. His cap was on straight. Its feather stood up, pointing to the blue Irish sky.

As they walked, they suddenly heard the footsteps and breathing of a human. "Watch out, Skiddley, lad," said the older one, quickly stepping behind a tall clump of shamrocks. "Don't let the likes of a human set eye on ye! Sure, and if one of the creatures can keep both eyes fixed on a leprechaun, with never a faltering glance, it's a known fact that the creature's got a power that the best magic of Erin can't withstand!"

"Fiddle-de-dee and fumbled frog legs, Broadwaller! Sure, and I've no fear of the human kind! Stupid oafs, I call them! I'll not hide from the likes of them!" And then young Skiddley jumped up on a log, turned a handspring, and sat down cross-legged to wait for the human to appear.

Before Broadwaller could say another word of warning, the nearby branches parted, and out stepped a burly, broad-middled man. He paused in surprise when he first saw Skiddley. But in just a moment his eyes narrowed, and he stepped toward the leprechaun. "Ah-ha! A true and trusty leprechaun, I do believe! Good morrow, young fellow! And where have you hidden the pot of gold that every leprechaun has in his keeping? It'll be mine now, lad, for everyone knows that when a leprechaun is caught, he has to give up his pot of gold. Where is it? Give it to me! Give it to me!"

"Fumbled frog legs, old man! You haven't caught me yet! Sure, and I'll not be telling the likes of you where my gold pot is! No, sir! I won't! Be off with you!" shouted Skiddley.

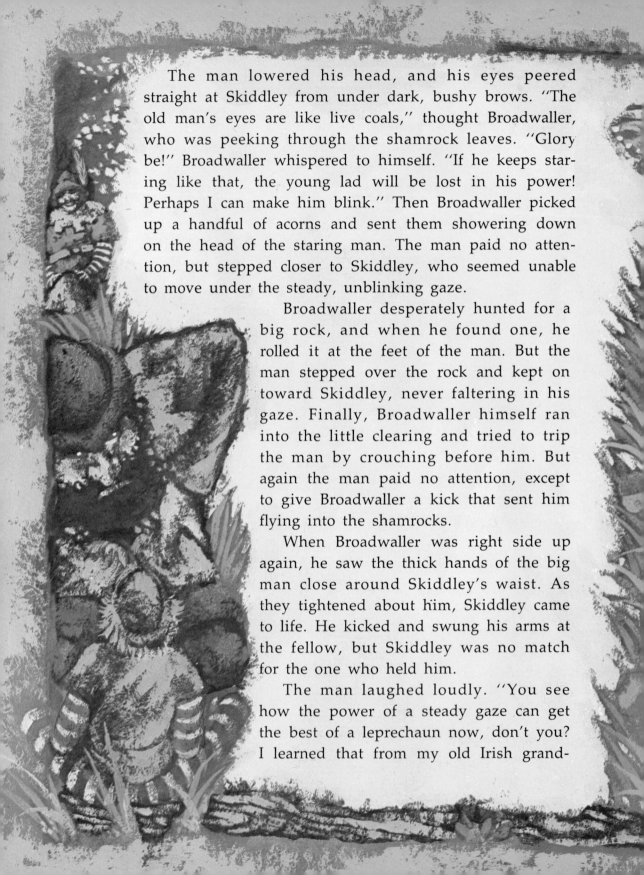

The man lowered his head, and his eyes peered straight at Skiddley from under dark, bushy brows. "The old man's eyes are like live coals," thought Broadwaller, who was peeking through the shamrock leaves. "Glory be!" Broadwaller whispered to himself. "If he keeps staring like that, the young lad will be lost in his power! Perhaps I can make him blink." Then Broadwaller picked up a handful of acorns and sent them showering down on the head of the staring man. The man paid no attention, but stepped closer to Skiddley, who seemed unable to move under the steady, unblinking gaze.

Broadwaller desperately hunted for a big rock, and when he found one, he rolled it at the feet of the man. But the man stepped over the rock and kept on toward Skiddley, never faltering in his gaze. Finally, Broadwaller himself ran into the little clearing and tried to trip the man by crouching before him. But again the man paid no attention, except to give Broadwaller a kick that sent him flying into the shamrocks.

When Broadwaller was right side up again, he saw the thick hands of the big man close around Skiddley's waist. As they tightened about him, Skiddley came to life. He kicked and swung his arms at the fellow, but Skiddley was no match for the one who held him.

The man laughed loudly. "You see how the power of a steady gaze can get the best of a leprechaun now, don't you? I learned that from my old Irish grand-

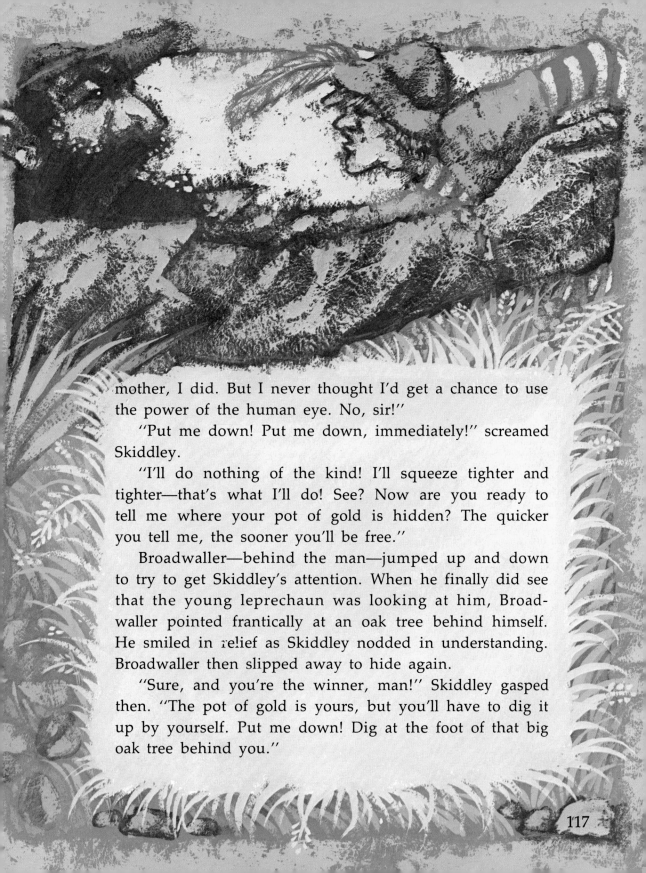

mother, I did. But I never thought I'd get a chance to use the power of the human eye. No, sir!"

"Put me down! Put me down, immediately!" screamed Skiddley.

"I'll do nothing of the kind! I'll squeeze tighter and tighter—that's what I'll do! See? Now are you ready to tell me where your pot of gold is hidden? The quicker you tell me, the sooner you'll be free."

Broadwaller—behind the man—jumped up and down to try to get Skiddley's attention. When he finally did see that the young leprechaun was looking at him, Broadwaller pointed frantically at an oak tree behind himself. He smiled in relief as Skiddley nodded in understanding. Broadwaller then slipped away to hide again.

"Sure, and you're the winner, man!" Skiddley gasped then. "The pot of gold is yours, but you'll have to dig it up by yourself. Put me down! Dig at the foot of that big oak tree behind you."

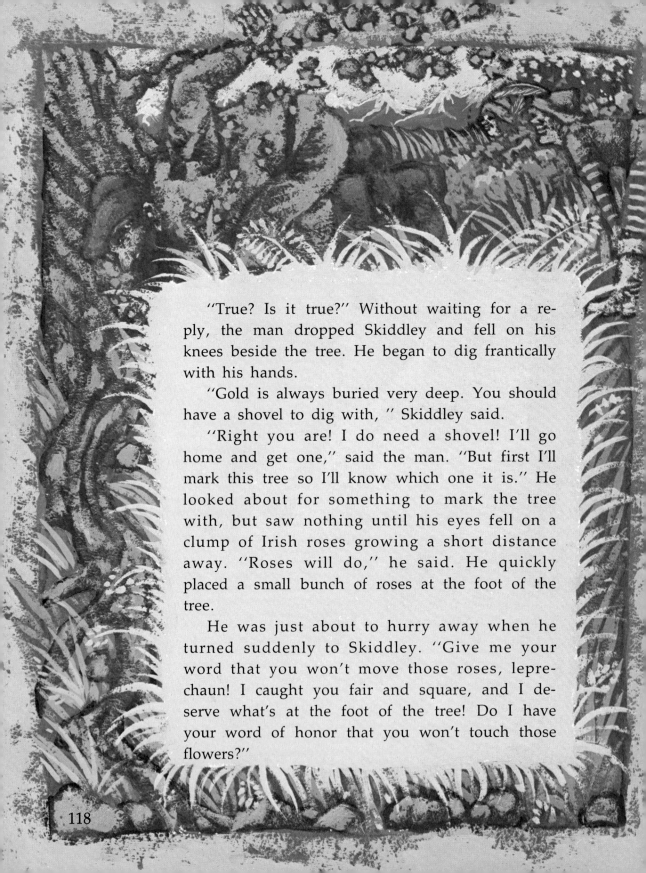

"True? Is it true?" Without waiting for a reply, the man dropped Skiddley and fell on his knees beside the tree. He began to dig frantically with his hands.

"Gold is always buried very deep. You should have a shovel to dig with, " Skiddley said.

"Right you are! I do need a shovel! I'll go home and get one," said the man. "But first I'll mark this tree so I'll know which one it is." He looked about for something to mark the tree with, but saw nothing until his eyes fell on a clump of Irish roses growing a short distance away. "Roses will do," he said. He quickly placed a small bunch of roses at the foot of the tree.

He was just about to hurry away when he turned suddenly to Skiddley. "Give me your word that you won't move those roses, leprechaun! I caught you fair and square, and I deserve what's at the foot of the tree! Do I have your word of honor that you won't touch those flowers?"

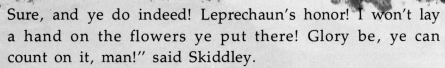

Sure, and ye do indeed! Leprechaun's honor! I won't lay a hand on the flowers ye put there! Glory be, ye can count on it, man!" said Skiddley.

With that, the man rushed off, and Broadwaller and Skiddley dropped to the ground and rolled with laughter. Then they picked handfuls of roses and put a few at the base of every oak tree in the clearing.

When they had finished, Broadwaller grinned. "Glory be!" he said with delight. "It would be a grand sight to see the face of that man when he finds all the trees marked with roses! It would, indeed!"

As they went on homeward, Skiddley said, "Sure, and I'm a wiser leprechaun than I was when we started this walk, Broadwaller, and I thank ye for your help." Then he skipped until the feather in his hat bobbed so hard it lifted the hat from his head.

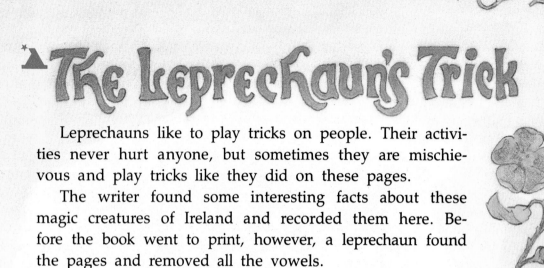

The Leprechaun's Trick

Leprechauns like to play tricks on people. Their activities never hurt anyone, but sometimes they are mischievous and play tricks like they did on these pages.

The writer found some interesting facts about these magic creatures of Ireland and recorded them here. Before the book went to print, however, a leprechaun found the pages and removed all the vowels.

Can you outsmart the leprechaun and still read the pages? Try it.

Write the sentences on a piece of paper. Fill in all the missing vowels. The lines within the words will give you a clue to the number of vowels missing.

Th__ L__ttl__ P____pl__ __f __r__l__nd

- L__pr__ch____ns __r__ l__ttl__ p____pl__ __f th__ __r__sh sp__r__t w__rld.
- Th____ __r__ m__rv__l____s sh____m__k__rs.
- S__m__ p____pl__ th__nk th____r n__m__ c__m__ fr__m th__ w__rds *leith bhrogen*, wh__ch m____n "th__ __n__ sh____m__k__r."
- Th____ __r__ __f sm__ll s__z__, n__v__r m__r__ th__n thr____ f____t t__ll.

- _ R__ss___n sc__nt__st b_l___v_s th_t s__ch cr___t__r_s r___ll_ __x__st_d.
- H_ b_l___v_s th_t th_ l_st _n_ _n _r_-l_nd d___d _n th_ s_v_nt___nth c_nt_r_.
- Th_ l_pr_ch___ns m_d_ sh___s c_nt_n___ll_ _nd b_c_m_ v_r_ r_ch.
- Th___ b_r___d th___r m_n___ _n tr___s_r_ cr__cks.
- H_ndr_ds _f t_l_s _b__t th_s_ l_ttl_ cr___t_r_s __x__st _n _r_l_nd.

Now try to find more information about the little people of Ireland in the library. Play the leprechaun's trick by writing several sentences on a sheet of paper and leaving out the vowels. Ask a friend to try to read it.

THE MONEY MACHINE

by Keith Robertson

Nell Lambert stepped through the front door onto the porch of the big, roomy, old-fashioned house at Number 202 Carson Street just in time to meet the mail. She was handed five letters and a small package. She put the letters on a table inside the door and, with the package in her hand, hurried across the yard to the carriage house. It was a neatly painted two-story building, the bottom floor of which served as a garage. Near one corner a narrow door opened onto a flight of steep stairs. Beside the door a white sign said CARSON STREET DETECTIVE AGENCY—SECOND FLOOR—WALK UP.

Nell bounded up the stairs three at a time and crossed the big loft to a battered desk. She sat down in an ancient swivel chair, searched for a pair of scissors in a desk drawer, and began to open the package.

Nell was a slender, dark-haired girl. There were wrinkles at the corners of her eyes, and her wide mouth seemed always ready to break into a grin. At the moment she was intent on the contents of her package. She removed the outer wrapping and carefully opened a small box. It held an odd-looking little machine with several rollers around which seemed to be wound strips of cloth. She placed this carefully on the top of her desk and unfolded the instructions.

THE FABULOUS MONEY MACHINE—INSTRUCTIONS, it said in big, bold, black letters and beneath, in slightly smaller type, Fool Your Friends—Have Fun at Parties—Mystify Everyone.

Nell hurried through the first two paragraphs, which were largely glowing words about what a wonderful machine she had purchased. The remaining instructions she read carefully. When she had finished, she got to

her feet and started to the stairs. Then she shook her head, returned to the desk, and carefully hid the machine in one of the big drawers. She returned to the house and found her mother, who was watering plants on the back porch. Like her daughter, Mrs. Lambert was slender, dark-haired, and quick of movement.

"I thought you said you were going over to Swede's," she said as Nell appeared.

"I was, but something came up," Nell said. "Could you let me have the five dollars I earned working in your garden?"

"I guess so," Mrs. Lambert said. "But I thought you wanted me to save it for you until you get enough to buy a tape recorder."

"I need it for an experiment."

"Well, it's your money," Mrs. Lambert said. "Would you go and get my purse from the hall table?"

Nell returned a moment later with the purse. Mrs. Lambert took out a five-dollar bill and handed it to her daughter.

"Thanks, Mom," Nell said. "I don't plan on spending it. I just want to use it for a while."

"That'll be interesting," said Mrs. Lambert. "I don't know how you use money without spending it."

"I just want to impress somebody," Nell said with a grin.

Nell returned to the hall and dialed Swede Larsen's number. She got Mrs. Larsen, who was unable to locate her son at the moment. So Nell left a message that Swede was to come over as soon as he was free. Then she hurried back to her office in the carriage house, took the fabulous money machine from the desk drawer, and placed it on the desk. She got out an old pair of scissors and, with the five-dollar bill as a guide, cut out a piece of paper exactly the same size as the bill.

Carefully following the instructions, she inserted the five-dollar bill between the two rolls and turned the knob on the side of the money machine. After a few turns the five-dollar bill disappeared completely, rolled up around one of the rollers. Next, Nell inserted the blank piece of paper at the other end and reversed the direction of the rollers. The paper disappeared and, as the final bit vanished, the five-dollar bill began to come out the other end. It was very convincing. It looked exactly as though

the blank piece of paper was being printed by the two rolls and was coming out as a nice, green, crisp five-dollar bill.

"Cool!" said Nell admiringly. "Real cool!"

She tried the trick several more times until she was certain how the machine worked. Then she carefully wound up the five-dollar bill and left it inside. She wadded up the blank piece of paper and tossed it in the wastepaper basket, put away the scissors, and waited impatiently for her friend Swede Larsen. Five minutes later there was the sound of bicycle tires on the gravel drive, followed by footsteps on the stairs. A husky, blond boy with blue eyes opened the door and crossed the room toward Nell.

"What's up?" he asked. "I thought you were coming over to my place."

"Well, I just invented a stupendous invention," Nell announced. "It's not patented yet so I don't want to carry it through the streets where everybody can see it."

"All right," said Swede, sitting on the corner of the desk. "What's the catch?"

"No catch," said Nell, slightly hurt. "It's just that genius has triumphed again. I have invented a money machine."

"Good!" said Swede. "And just in time. I'm so broke I was about to take a job with Mrs. Kimball cleaning out her cellar. Believe me, anyone willing to work for Mrs. Kimball is desperate."

"Work will no longer be necessary," said Nell with a grand wave of her hand. She reached into the desk and took out a blank piece of paper and scissors. "Now, just cut a piece of paper the size of a five-dollar bill."

The Demonstration

Swede picked up the piece of paper and the scissors and glanced at her doubtfully. "It's been so long since I've had five dollars, I've forgotten what a five-dollar bill looks like," he said. "But I'll try."

He cut a rectangular piece of paper from the sheet and handed it to Nell.

"It looks a little big," Nell said judiciously. "And one end isn't square. People are fussy about their money, you know."

She opened the lower drawer of the desk and took out the money machine. Carefully she inserted the white piece of paper and turned the knobs. The five-dollar bill came rolling out the other end.

"Neat," said Swede, picking up the five-dollar bill. "That's a real smooth trick. Where'd you get it?"

"I invented it," Nell insisted. "It's no trick at all."

"Don't put me on!" Swede said, reaching for the machine.

Nell was too quick for him and moved it out of his reach.

"As I said," she explained, "it isn't patented yet. Of course, I would sell you a half interest in it for a reasonable amount."

"Like what?" Swede asked.

"Oh, a dollar and a half," Nell replied.

"It's a deal," Swede said. He held out the five-dollar bill. "Have you got three and a half dollars change?"

"Change, my eye! That's my five-dollar bill."

"Why?" asked Swede. "I cut out the paper, didn't I? And the paper belonged to the Carson Street Detective Agency, which makes it mine as much as yours. Besides, with this wonderful machine you can just print yourself another."

"All right," said Nell. "Give me back the five, and I'll show you how it works." She demonstrated the machine twice, and then Swede tried it.

"Not bad," he said finally. "Not bad at all. Where did you get it?"

"I sent off to that firm in Wisconsin. You know, the one that has the catalog with the tricks and magic. It cost three dollars."

"OK," said Swede. "I'll purchase half interest for a dollar and a half. Only you're going to have to trust me for the money for a while."

"A dollar seventy-five," said Nell. "There was fifty cents postage."

"All right," said Swede. "I'd just as soon owe you a dollar seventy-five as a dollar and a half, anyhow." He looked at the machine thoughtfully. "We've got to go pull it on someone. Eileen?"

Nell shook her head. Eileen was Swede's younger sister. "No," she said. "Eileen is not as dumb as she used to be. She'd know we couldn't print five-dollar bills, and she'd pester us until she found out how it worked. Then she'd tell everybody. We ought to pick somebody real dumb."

They were silent for several minutes. Then suddenly Swede snapped his fingers and said, "I've got it. Solid State O'Brien should be at the soda fountain down at Heckleberry's drugstore."

"He'd be perfect!" Nell agreed enthusiastically. "Let's put the five-dollar bill back in the machine and make certain that we're all set. Do you think it's better to take the pieces of paper all cut or to cut them right there at the soda fountain?"

"I think we ought to take half a dozen or so all cut to size," Swede said judiciously. "We can act as though we go around almost anywhere printing five-dollar bills."

Ten minutes later they were seated at the soda fountain in Heckleberry's drugstore. Their visit was timed perfectly. It was early enough in the afternoon that there was little soda-fountain trade. They had the undivided attention of the young man behind the counter. Solid State O'Brien had been christened Michael. He was a pleasant-faced young man, three or four years older than Nell and Swede. His wide, blue eyes looked believingly upon the world, and everything he saw was new that day and wonderful. He was friendly and likable, and although he had made thousands of sodas, banana splits, and sundaes, he made each new order with enthusiasm and dash as though he enjoyed making it. He was also generous with the ice cream, which made him popular, too. When it came to adding up the check and making change, he was not quite so outstanding.

Solid State took their order and in less than a minute had placed two beautiful, oversized sundaes in front of them.

"Hey, have you got any money?" Nell asked suddenly, pausing before consuming the last spoonful of ice cream.

"I thought you had the money," Swede said.

"One of you better have some money," Solid State O'Brien said with a warning note in his voice. "It is strictly cash at this fountain."

"Why don't you write a check?" Nell suggested.

Swede ate the last of his sundae and appeared to consider the suggestion. "No," he said finally. "I don't think I want to write a check. Why don't we just print some money?"

"Good idea," said Nell. "Have you got the machine with you?"

"It's in the box right here at my feet," said Swede. He leaned down, picked up the box, opened it, and set the money machine on the soda-fountain counter.

"Got any paper?" Nell asked Solid State.

"What kind of paper?" Solid State asked suspiciously.

"Oh, a good grade of paper," Nell replied casually.

"You have to use good paper when you print money. I'd like a pair of scissors, too, so I can cut it to the right size."

"What are you two trying to pull?" Solid State asked.

"You'd think he didn't want to be paid," Nell said.

"Well, if he doesn't want to cooperate, we can get along without him," Swede said. "I've got some paper in my pocket." He took out one of the slips that they had cut before leaving their headquarters. "As a matter of fact, it looks as though it's just about the right size."

Solid State moved over until he was just a few feet away. He looked down at the box suspiciously. Nell started to take the machine out of the box, but Swede held out a warning hand.

"I'm not so sure we should do this right in front of Solid State," he said doubtfully. "After all, it hasn't been patented yet."

"I don't think Solid State would try to steal our invention. Besides, no one's going to figure this out just from watching it once or twice. And we do have to pay for the sundaes."

"OK," said Swede.

Solid State leaned over the counter and watched intently as Swede fed the piece of paper into the rollers and Nell turned the crank. His eyes showed surprise as a crisp five-dollar bill slowly emerged from the other end.

He looked at the machine and then from Nell to Swede and back to the machine again.

"Here you are," Swede said, handing him the five-dollar bill.

"You expect me to cash that?" Solid State asked incredulously. "You're crazy!"

"Why?" Nell asked. "What's wrong with it?"

Hook, Line, and Sinker

Solid State took the five-dollar bill and gingerly turned it from one side to the other, examining it carefully. Had he been a little bit more observing, he would have noticed that, although the bill was crisp and rather new, it did show some signs of wear. Obviously, it had been in someone's wallet before. It was certainly not as clean and unwrinkled as the piece of paper Swede had put into the machine.

"Well?" Swede asked, putting the machine back in the box and closing the lid. "Are you going to stand there or give us our change?"

"I don't think I'd better," said Solid State doubtfully.

"All right," said Nell agreeably, reaching over and plucking the bill from Solid State's fingers. "I suppose

133

you'll trust us long enough for me to go next door and get it changed?"

Solid State nodded dumbly.

Nell hurried out and down the street two doors to a record-and-card shop where she knew the owner. She had the bill changed into five ones and returned to the drugstore. She held the five one-dollar bills out where they could be seen clearly, peeled off one, and plunked it down on the soda fountain.

"With some people, not even seeing is believing," she said with her nose in the air. "Mr. Osborne gave me five ones for my five without any questions. I'd like some change please."

Solid State picked up the one-dollar bill and, shaking his head doubtfully, went to the cash register to ring up the sale of the two sundaes. He returned and placed thirty cents on the soda-fountain counter. Nell promptly picked it up and stuck it in her pocket.

"And after all the trouble you've caused us, if you think we're going to leave you a tip, you're out of your tree."

"You guys never leave me a tip, anyhow," Solid State grumbled.

Swede picked up the box with the money machine and stuck it under his arm. Together, he and Nell walked to the door.

"Don't take any wooden nickels," Swede called back to Solid State.

Solid State was still staring after them with disbelief as they disappeared from sight. As soon as they were well clear of the drugstore, they broke into wild laughter.

"He fell for that hook, line, and sinker," Nell said, when she was finally able to talk.

"We put on quite an act," Swede agreed. "I think we ought to go on the stage. We could print money and throw bills out to the audience."

"Not me," said Nell. "Any money that comes out of that machine was ours to begin with, and I'm not throwing it out to anyone."

The school year was almost over. The Wednesday following their act with the money machine, classes were dismissed early. Swede and Nell walked leisurely back toward Nell's house. They were climbing the stairs of the carriage house to the Carson Street Detective Agency headquarters when Mrs. Lambert called to Nell from the back porch.

"There was a gentleman here looking for you this afternoon," she said. "I told him you were in school, and he said he would be back about four o'clock."

"What was his name?" Nell called.

"LeBon," Mrs. Lambert replied.

"I don't know anybody by that name," Nell said. "What did he want?"

"Why don't you come here so I won't have to shout," Mrs. Lambert suggested. Nell and Swede strolled to within a few feet of the back porch.

"He was a man in his late forties or early fifties," Mrs. Lambert explained. "Short and sort of stocky, with short gray hair. He was very pleasant and polite. First he asked if you lived here, and I said that you did and that I was your mother, and he then wanted to know how old you were. He was sort of surprised when I told him that you were in junior high school."

Nell shook her head. "I haven't any idea who he is."

"Well, there was something official-looking about him," Mrs. Lambert said. "He didn't say, but I got the idea he was a state or federal official."

"Probably the FBI," Nell said airily. "They've heard of our detective agency and have come to us for help."

"Yes, I'm sure that's it," Mrs. Lambert agreed dryly.

"Well, tell him to come on up to the office when he shows up," Nell said.

They climbed the stairs to the office. Back of the battered desk was a row of shelves made of orange crates stacked one on top of another. The shelves were filled with an assortment of junk. One shelf was marked SECRET—KEEP OUT and another CODE SECTION—CONFIDENTIAL.

"You know," Nell said thoughtfully, looking around the room, "this office is pretty crumby."

"Agreed," admitted Swede. "What we need is a nice carpet on the floor, a couple of new executive-type desks, and some new swivel chairs."

"And a stereo set," Nell added.

"That's right," agreed Swede. "There's nothing like music to make you relax, and that's just what I'm going to do right now, music or no music." He sat down in an ancient chair and put his feet up on the desk.

Nell opened the window for some fresh air and then joined her friend, drawing up a second chair to the desk.

"School will be out next week," Swede said. "What a beautiful thought."

"Yes, it is," agreed Nell. "But while I wouldn't want anyone in school to hear me, I'm going to sort of miss school this summer. I haven't got anything planned."

"Neither have I," said Swede. "I suppose I'll work

some around home and part-time for my father. What we need is a really good mystery to solve."

"That's right," Nell agreed. "There hasn't been a decent crime in months now."

"Criminals have no imagination anymore," Swede said seriously. "All they do is simple things like hold up a grocery store. And they scatter clues all around so that even the dumbest police officer in the world could solve it without half trying."

"I guess we were born a couple of hundred years too late," Nell said sadly. "Crime used to be more interesting in the old days."

"How so?" Swede asked.

"Well, just look at highway robbers, for example," Nell observed. "They went around on horses and held up stagecoaches with rich nobles in them and carried off beautiful women passengers. Now what does a highway robber do today? Highjacks a truck full of underwear or something just as bad."

"You're right," agreed Swede. "There's been an awful comedown. Just look at piracy. Think of all the swashbuckling pirates that used to swarm through the Caribbean. Ships were full of gold in the old days. Now what would happen if you captured a ship? It would probably be full of machinery, and you wouldn't know what to do with it."

"What's probably going to happen is that crime is going to get so uninteresting that it's going to vanish from the face of the earth," said Nell despondently.

"I doubt it," said a voice from the door.

Startled, they looked around to discover a short, stocky, gray-haired man standing at the top of the stairs.

The Case Is Closed

"Are you Nell Lambert and Swede Larsen?" he asked.

"Guilty," said Nell.

"I hope not," said the man, coming in.

Nell got up and offered the visitor her chair. She sat down on a box herself.

"I'm Henry LeBon," said the man.

"He's Swede, and I'm Nell," said Nell, pointing to Swede with her thumb. "What can we do for you, Mr. LeBon?"

"Well, my department had a tip that you two were engaged in some rather questionable activities," Mr. LeBon said.

"Questionable?" Nell asked, sitting up.

"Well, illegal is probably a better word," said Mr. LeBon with a slight smile.

"I don't know of anything illegal that we've done," Nell said. "We haven't even parked our bicycles in the wrong spot."

"I'm with the Secret Service," said Mr. LeBon pleasantly. "To come right to the heart of the matter, we received a report that you two have been counterfeiting."

Nell and Swede looked at each other in amazement, and then both had the same thought at the same time. They stared at each other in disbelief.

"Solid State!" Swede said finally. "That lunkhead!"

"Did Solid State tell you that we were counterfeiting, Mr. LeBon?"

Mr. LeBon raised one eyebrow. "I'm afraid that you've lost me," he said. "What is this solid-state business?"

"Solid State is that lunkhead that works in Heckleberry's drugstore," said Nell. "His head is solid bone, so everybody calls him Solid State. Is he the one who told you we were counterfeiting?"

Mr. LeBon nodded with a slight smile. "He said you two had a machine and were printing money right in front of his eyes. I had my doubts on the matter, and then, when I came up and found out that you were both still in junior high school, I was even more skeptical. While I was waiting to talk to you, I went down and spent an hour or so with Chief Bricker of your local police force. He tells me that you two are reasonably law-abiding citizens, and, in fact, have helped solve some crimes."

"We didn't actually print any money," Nell said. "Wait a moment, and I'll show you." She opened the desk drawer and got out the money machine. She placed it on top of the desk and then got a piece of paper from the drawer.

"The trouble with this machine," she admitted, "is that you can't make it work unless you have some paper money in the first place, and I haven't got any. Swede, have you got a dollar bill?"

"Are you out of your mind?" Swede asked.

Mr. LeBon reached into his pocket and brought out a billfold. He produced a one-dollar bill.

"Will this help?" he asked.

"Well, it's more convincing if the bill's newer," Nell said. "But we'll have to make do."

She fed the bill into the machine and then, when it was all set, turned to Mr. LeBon. "You understand, you do all this ahead of time. When we went into Heckleberry's, the machine was loaded with a five-dollar bill. We did a lot of talking about printing money, and finally we fed a slip of plain paper into the machine, like this." She turned the knob, and out the other end came the one-dollar bill that Mr. LeBon had supplied.

LeBon chuckled. "That looks quite realistic," he said. "Let me see it."

Nell pushed the machine across the desk top, and LeBon examined it carefully. He turned the knob several times and did the trick himself.

"I think I'll have to get one of these and take it back to Washington with me," he said. "We've got some people gullible enough down there that I might convince them. Just as you did this Solid State boy."

"You didn't come all the way from Washington just to investigate us, did you?" Nell asked in amazement.

"Not really," admitted LeBon. "Actually, had it been just this single report, I think I could have found out over the telephone that it was a false alarm. But you see, we have been having trouble with counterfeit bills being passed in this area."

"Really?" asked Swede, sitting up with interest.

"You mean right here in town?" Nell asked.

"Right in the area, I'm sorry to say," said Mr. LeBon. "We had warned the merchants in this area to be on the lookout for counterfeit twenty-dollar bills. I suppose your friend Solid State was among those warned. That's how he happened to tip us off so promptly about your activities."

"This is just the sort of case that the Carson Street Detective Agency specializes in," Nell said with a grin. "Maybe we can help you."

"Maybe you can," agreed Mr. LeBon. "I can use some help. There seems to be a fairly widespread ring of counterfeiters. Through little bits of information here and there, we have reason to believe that their headquarters may be somewhere in this general area."

"It must be exciting to be in the Secret Service," Nell said.

"Well, I've liked it, or I wouldn't have spent thirty years in it," said Mr. LeBon with a slight smile. "But there's more plain drudgery in catching a criminal than there is exciting action. And it seems that you just get to the bottom of one counterfeit plot and break up a ring when you have another. That's why I said that I doubted if crime was vanishing from the face of the earth."

He got to his feet.

"There's nothing illegal about using this machine as a joke, is there?" Swede asked.

"No," admitted LeBon. "But do me a favor. After you've demonstrated it, tell whomever you've pulled a trick on that it's a joke. It will save us from answering a lot of excited calls."

Mr. LeBon disappeared down the stairs.

Nell sat down and drew a deep breath.

"You wouldn't think even Solid State would be that stupid," Swede said, shaking his head.

"Yes, I would," said Nell. "But what's really amazing is that there's a counterfeiting ring right here in town."

"He didn't say in town," Swede disagreed. "He said in the general area."

"All right, in the general area," Nell said. "That's our summer project. Break up the counterfeiting ring. Just imagine sneaking up on their headquarters and finding a whole satchelful of nice fresh money—maybe a million dollars."

"And all of it counterfeit," Swede said sourly. "A lot of good that would do us."

"Well, maybe there'd be a reward. Anyhow, I think we ought to try to solve the case."

"I'm agreeable," said Swede. "All we need to do is figure out how to start."

Nell reached over and picked up the money machine Mr. LeBon had examined. She turned the crank, and out came a one-dollar bill. "Hey, we're already making money on this case," she said happily. "He forgot to take his dollar bill."

"We better look at it closely. It might be counterfeit," Swede warned.

They examined the one-dollar bill carefully, but it seemed to be genuine.

"He may come back," Nell said. "I think we better enter it in the books as a retainer fee from the Secret Service."

Magic Money Trick

You can make money appear without having the fabulous money machine like Nell Lambert did.

Get a clear plastic glass, one sheet of white unlined paper, scissors, glue, one dime, and one handkerchief.

Do these steps before you gather your friends:

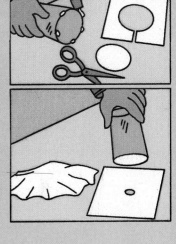

- Place the plastic glass on one half of the paper, trace around the rim of the glass, and cut out the drawing so that no pencil marks are visible.
- Put small amounts of glue on the rim of the glass, and carefully place the cut-out circle on the rim of the glass. Be sure to let the glue dry.
- Place a dime on the other half of the paper.
- Place the plastic glass with the paper side down on the dime.

Now you are ready to practice the magic trick. You will ask your friends to look through the glass to see if they see anything, which they won't. Then you will tell them that you can make a coin appear. Put a handkerchief over the glass and say the magic word *abracadabra*. Keeping the handkerchief over the glass, pick up the glass. Your friends will see a dime.

Practice the trick until you can do it well. Then gather your friends for the performance. You will look like a master magician.

145

Money Madne$$

Q: If a parent gives one child fifteen cents and another child ten cents, what time will it be?

A: A quarter to two

Q: If I had a $100 bill in one coat pocket and a $100 bill in the other coat pocket, what would I have?

A: Someone else's coat

Q: There used to be gold coins as well as paper money. A $20 gold piece had twice as much gold in it as a $10 gold piece, and both were pure gold. Which would be worth more: half a pound of $20 gold pieces or a pound of $10 gold pieces?

A: A pound of gold is worth more than half a pound.

146

Q: What is the difference between a crazy rabbit and a counterfeit ten-dollar bill?

A: One's a mad bunny, and the other is bad money.

Q: Why is paper money more valuable than coins?

A: When you put it in your pocket, you double it, and when you take it out, you find it in creases.

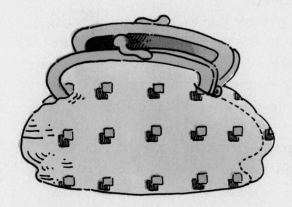

Q: Why is an empty purse always the same?

A: Because there's never any change in it

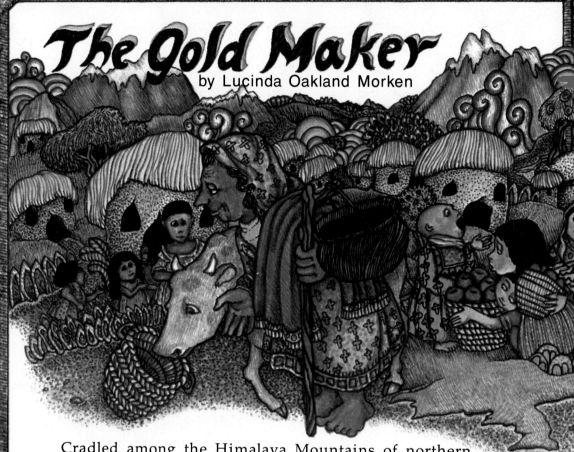

The Gold Maker

by Lucinda Oakland Morken

Cradled among the Himalaya Mountains of northern India, the sleepy village hardly stirred when a little old woman limped in from the east.

Without a glance, she passed the thatched mud huts, the poorly clad people sitting by their doorways, and the saffron-robed, shaved priests.

A cow—sacred in India—stopped, blocking the pathway while it took its time sniffing the bottom of an empty basket.

The stranger waited patiently. She shifted the red blanket on her shoulder and the iron kettle she carried on a stick.

The cow decided to spend the night right there and settled down, almost blocking the street.

The old woman carefully made her way around it and on to the little square, where travelers could build fires and cook their suppers.

She made a fire of cow chips and hung her kettle with a little water in it over the flame. When the water started boiling, she took a big handful of mud and dumped it into the kettle. Then she started stirring with her stick.

Curious children crowded around her. "What are you doing?" one asked.

"I am making gold," the little woman answered.

A few villagers moved closer, chuckling. The old woman paid no attention to them but went on stirring and stirring in the kettle.

Finally, she finished and dumped her kettle full of boiled mud on the ground. She poked around in it with the stick. Sure enough, there lay a lump of gold, the size of a bean.

The villagers stared at one another. "Is it real gold?" someone asked.

Brown hands reached out and examined the shiny, small lump. "It is real" was the general opinion.

The little woman just sat cross-legged, staring into space, till someone put the gold back into the kettle and set it down beside her.

Evening came. The silver-haired monkeys stopped their chattering in the treetops. A big yellow moon shone over the snow-covered mountains.

The old brown woman wrapped her blanket around her and lay down on the ground beside her kettle.

"Hsst! Hsst!" Someone whispered over her shoulder. It was Thakoor, the only rich one in the village. "Show me how to make gold, and I will give you 500 rupees," he said.

"Do you think I am such a fool that I would sell my secret for a mere 500 rupees?" the old woman replied.

Thakoor raised his offer. The old woman shook her head. Finally, Thakoor said, "I'll give you 1,000 rupees—all I own."

But the answer was still no.

The sun rose over the glittering snow on the mountaintops the next morning. The old woman rose, cooked her rice in the iron kettle, and slowly ate her breakfast.

Then she made a fresh fire and started her gold-making again. News of her doings spread through the village faster than a thatch fire in a strong wind. Children swarmed around her. Their parents all but pushed them aside to get closer to the kettle. Everyone in the village wanted to learn how to make gold.

The little old woman stirred and stirred and stirred. Finally a small lump of shining gold appeared in the mud which she was cooking. It was slightly larger than yesterday's lump.

The crowd grew excited.

While the villagers were exclaiming to one another over this miracle, the council members met and decided that the village as a whole ought to benefit from the old woman's wonderful secret. Naturally, Thakoor was their leader.

Within an hour, the villagers had put all their money into the public treasury. The sum came to exactly 5,000 rupees.

Respectfully, they gathered again at the square where the old woman was resting on her blanket, watching the monkeys in the treetops.

When the villagers offered her 5,000 rupees for her secret, the woman closed her eyes and sank into deep thought.

Finally, she opened her eyes and placed her stick in the hand of the rich one, Thakoor. "Stir without stopping, and gold will form," she said. "There is only one thing you must not do. You must not think about brown monkeys. If you should happen to think of brown monkeys while you are stirring, no gold will form."

The woman accepted the 5,000 rupees, placed them in a leather bag at her waist, picked up her blanket and kettle, and limped slowly down the road to the west.

Eagerly the rich one brought a kettle, built a fire, and stirred and stirred. However, the thought of brown monkeys popped into his head. Try as he would, he could think of nothing else. Finally, he gave up.

Another villager took a turn, with the same result. Another and then another villager tried to make gold. Always after a few minutes, each would give up, exclaiming that brown monkeys would not stay out of their thoughts.

If you should visit this tiny poverty-stricken village high in the Himalayas, you might find a tired villager or two, still stirring and trying very hard not to think about brown monkeys.

Money Sayings

A proverb is a short, wise saying used for a long time by a lot of people. Some proverbs are based on fact, and some are just personal opinion. Others are a combination of fact and opinion.

Below are some proverbs related to money matters.

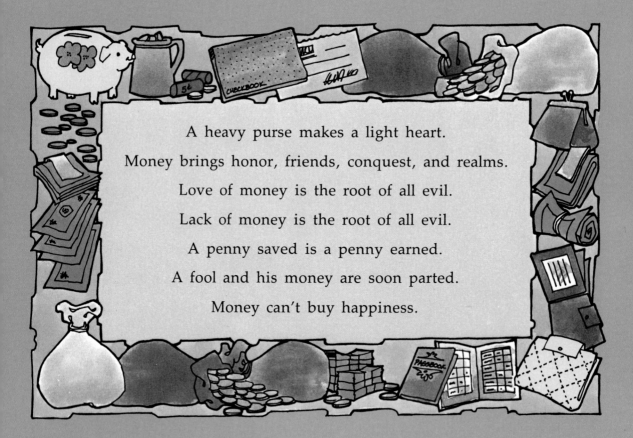

A heavy purse makes a light heart.

Money brings honor, friends, conquest, and realms.

Love of money is the root of all evil.

Lack of money is the root of all evil.

A penny saved is a penny earned.

A fool and his money are soon parted.

Money can't buy happiness.

Which proverbs might apply to "The Gold Maker"? Explain their meaning and how they relate to the story.

California Gold

by Barbara Friedmann and Jennifer Phelps

CHARACTERS

JAMES WILSON MARSHALL MRS. MARSHALL

PROSPECTOR REPORTER PROSPECTOR'S WIFE

SCENE ONE

SETTING: *Beside a stream at Sutter's Mill in California*

REPORTER (*With microphone in hand, addressing the audience*): Good afternoon, everyone, and welcome to our show *You Were There*. Today we will be going back to the year 1849 and will be joining James Wilson Marshall at Sutter's Mill in California. James Wilson Marshall was the first to discover gold in this stream and is now panning for gold with another prospector. (*He walks over to James Wilson Marshall and the prospector as they are panning for gold.*) Tell us, Mr. Marshall, do you think you'll find gold today?

JAMES MARSHALL (*Immersing a pan in the stream, then lifting the pan and swirling the water again and again*): I hope so, but using this pan is such a slow way to look for gold. After all, I can work with only one round pan and take only one dip in the stream at a time.

PROSPECTOR (*Panning for gold next to Marshall*): It also takes a long time to swirl the water over and over to wash away all the gravel and mud and leave just the gold at the bottom.

REPORTER: Mr. Marshall, can you tell us how panning for gold ever got started?

JAMES MARSHALL: I remember it very clearly. I just happened to be getting some water from this very stream to wash my face, back in January 1848. When I finished and started to throw the leftover water back into the stream, I noticed these little shiny rocks in the bottom of my pan. Was I excited! It turned out to be gold.

REPORTER: You were lucky, too! Ever since you found that gold, people have been rushing to California to look for their own gold and to strike it rich.

JAMES MARSHALL: But I still think that I can come up with a faster way to separate the gravel and the mud from the gold in the stream water. I've been thinking about an idea that might work. I could build a big box to pour the stream water into and put a tiny opening in

one end of the box. Then, when the water pours out of the box, all the gold ore will be trapped at the opening. (*He turns to the prospector, who continues to pan for gold.*) What do you think of that idea?

PROSPECTOR: I think it'll work. It would sure save us a lot of time and make it possible to find a lot more gold.

REPORTER (*Walking away from the men and talking to the audience*): While the men discuss their plans to find a new gadget for panning for gold, let's interview the women to get their reactions to the gold rush.

SCENE TWO

SETTING: *In the kitchen of a pioneer cabin*

REPORTER: Mrs. Marshall, the news of your husband's discovery of gold is spreading rapidly, and people are flocking to California, hoping to find their claim. Do you see much change taking place in your town?

MRS. MARSHALL: Oh my, yes. I went into San Francisco to get some supplies yesterday. You wouldn't believe how many people are coming to California to find gold. There just aren't enough places for all the people to stay!

REPORTER: I heard that the town is growing quite fast.

MRS. MARSHALL: That's right. And you wouldn't believe the high prices for food and supplies! There is so little food, and so much gold, that prices are sky-high. Why, a small shack is even renting for $100 a week! But people don't seem to mind paying that much.

PROSPECTOR'S WIFE: Why should they mind? They think they can get all the gold they need to pay for it. I heard that they are starting to ship supplies by water now. They bring ships from the east coast down around the tip of South America and then all the way up the west coast to San Francisco.

REPORTER: That must take a very long time. Of course, coming across America by covered wagon took a long time, too.

MRS. MARSHALL: People are coming to California, hoping to find gold and strike it rich. However, not too many of them are striking it rich. Some people are becoming discouraged and are turning back. (*Sighing*) I just hope all those people find jobs so that they can pay for food and supplies. If they can, then gold will have been an important beginning for California.

(*James Marshall and the prospector enter the house, carrying a clumsy-looking box.*)

REPORTER: Well, men, how's work on the new gadget coming along?

MR. MARSHALL: I think it'll work.

MRS. MARSHALL (*Interrupting*): What kind of gadget is that?

PROSPECTOR: Your husband has come up with a new way for us to pan for gold.

JAMES MARSHALL: That's right. I've been experimenting again. I've made a big box with a small hole in it. It's really nothing more than a giant pan. I figure it can do the work of at least thirty men with their little pans.

PROSPECTOR: That means we can find thirty times as much gold!

PROSPECTOR'S WIFE: Well, I hope so. Some people have spent so much and have received so little in return.

PROSPECTOR: I know it'll work. After all, everything else James has made has worked.

JAMES MARSHALL: The idea behind it is certainly sound, and if it does work, we'll be able to go to other areas and other streams to look for gold. Who knows? There might even be some places out here in the West that have more gold than Sutter's Mill.

(The women continue to discuss the changes that are taking place in their town, and the men go to work on the new gadget. The reporter walks away, leaving them in the background, and talks to the audience.)

REPORTER: Well, ladies and gentlemen, that's our live report from Sutter's Mill in California. Throughout the coming year, prospectors, called forty-niners, will continue to settle in the small town of San Francisco and will stake their claims. Soon many of them will be using a big wooden box that will separate gravel and mud from the gold in a short time. The miners who find gold will make a flourishing town of San Francisco. Within a year's time, the small town will grow to a city of 25,000 people. Even miners who aren't lucky will stay in California and become farmers and ranchers. By 1850 California will have a population of 93,000—more than the 60,000 required to be admitted as a state.

That's our program for today. Join us again for *You Were There*, when we will take you behind the scenes and on the spot for more historical interviews.

A Golden Opportunity

Imagine how James Wilson Marshall felt when he discovered gold in California. Although he tried to keep the discovery a secret for a while, the news leaked out. Soon people from all over the world were rushing to California for an opportunity to make their claim and strike it rich.

Pretend that you are a newspaper reporter at the time of the discovery. Your assignment is to write a story about the discovery of gold in California. To help you write the story, do the following:

- Think about what you are going to write.
- Write a catchy headline for your story.
- Use facts from the play *California Gold*. Then find additional facts about the California gold rush in other books or the encyclopedia.
- Write the story.
- Draw or find pictures to accompany your story.

Remember that a good reporter answers the 5 W's—who, what, where, when, and why. To help you do this, you may include answers to some of the following questions:

- When and where does the story take place?
- Who are the people in the story?
- How was the gold discovered?
- What outstanding qualities does gold possess that have made it so valuable?
- Why did people come from all over the world to make their claim?
- What were some of the people's reactions to the discovery of gold?
- How has life changed for the people in California since the discovery?
- What are some of the changes that you see taking place in the future, as a result of the discovery?

When you draw the picture, be sure that the picture is about something that you described in the story—maybe James Wilson Marshall's new gadget for finding gold, or a map showing the place of the discovery of gold.

After you have written your story and drawn your picture, share them with your friends.

Would your story receive a Gold Medal for reporting?

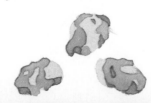

Books for You

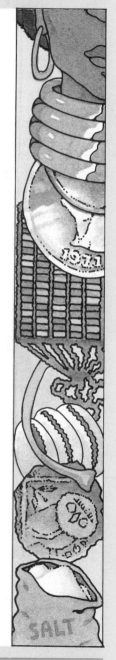

Nickels, Dimes, and Dollars by Ronald V. Fodor

If you are interested in knowing more about the history of money, how it is manufactured and circulated, and how money works in foreign markets, then this book is for you.

Run for the Money by Scott Corbett

Would you make a good detective? Read this story to see if you can solve the mystery.

The Hundred Penny Box by Sharon Bell Mathis

Aunt Dew, Michael's great-great-aunt, has a hundred penny box in which she has saved one penny for each year of her life. Michael becomes Aunt Dew's protector when his mother wants to dispose of the box of pennies.

Managing Your Money by Elizabeth James and Carol Barkin

Learn how to handle your personal finances by reading about savings and checking accounts, credit cards, and budgets.

Jason and the Money Tree by Sonia Levitin

Jason's grandfather left Jason a ten-dollar bill when he died. Jason thinks that the bill has significance. He even dreams that he plants the bill and it takes root and blooms. Jason, feeling a little foolish about believing a dream, plants the bill.

Remembrance of Things Past

by Robert Hays

It was a warm, sticky evening, typically humid for east Texas in mid-May. Even though sundown was still a half hour away, the lights of Kate Ross Barr Memorial Park had been turned on. Four games in the Huntsville Summer Youth League were in progress.

On the baseball fields, boys in three different age divisions were playing. The girls played softball on Field 4. Two evenly matched Pony League teams were in the fifth inning on the field in front of me, the game tied. My son was coming to bat.

From behind, the bleacher fans at Field 4 cheered wildly. One of the girls' teams had a big inning going. I turned and looked that way. One of the girls was chasing a ball in center field. Two girls, in their bright red tee shirts and white shorts, were racing around the bases.

In my mind I went back, twenty, twenty-five years, even beyond that. Back to southern Illinois, to a time and place where we played ball and our parents cheered much the same as those I heard around me now. It seemed such a short time ago—but how different.

Our sports were basketball, some softball, and track and field, too. There was no organized summer-league activity, but during the school months we played hard at team sports.

Ours was a one-room country school called Walnut Grove. There was a church by the same name, but most of the community activity centered around the school. We had Christmas programs and Halloween parties and any other affairs we could think of to bring all the kids and parents together like one big, happy family.

Not that the family was all that big. In a good year we had thirty-six students at Walnut Grove, including first through eighth graders.

So sometimes it was hard to get enough "big kids"—anyone from the third grade up qualified as a "big kid"—to make up a softball team. It only took five for basketball. Maybe our uniforms were a little shabby, compared to today's double knits, but we took our sports just as seriously. For us, the White County Grade School Basketball Tournament was the NCAA finals and the NBA playoffs all rolled into one.

We wanted our best five players out there. It never really occurred to us that some of us were boys and some were girls. We were a team representing Walnut Grove, and we played to win.

Thinking back, I remembered the strength some of the girls brought to the team. I thought of Nina, with her speed and quickness. She was a clutch player, the kind you went to with time running out in a tight game.

Joan was younger and more of a battler. She never developed the finesse, but she made up for that in effort and determination. Today we'd call it hustle.

I remembered Marilyn, too. Always small for her age. She got more bench time than playing time, but she played when she had the chance, and she loved it. I remembered her now, not for her performance, but for her shoes.

At Walnut Grove our equipment was limited. The school would buy what we needed, but most of us were poor kids not accustomed to too much. We had uniforms and shoes that almost fit. Marilyn's feet were pretty small, and her basketball shoes were pretty big.

This particular game was turning into a lopsided win. Marilyn got to play more than usual that night. Everybody noticed. When she ran back and forth from one end of the floor to the other, her too-large shoes "plop-plop-plopped" with every step. The sound echoed across the court, and people began to laugh. But Marilyn never seemed to mind. She got to play a whole quarter of that game.

We had no reason to consider our team unusual. Most of the rural schools—and there were still plenty of them—had "unisex" teams (although the word wasn't around then and, anyway, no one would have thought of using such a word). None of these schools had gyms. We practiced and played on outdoor courts.

During the winter months, early morning was always a good time for practice, even in wet weather. The ground was frozen then, hard and smooth. If we played too long, the bare surface began to melt as the sun got higher, and the court got sloppy. We usually played too long, but that was a good time to improve our passing game, even though it was difficult to dribble on the soft, muddy surface.

Still, many of our games were against schools in neighboring towns with gyms and all-boy teams. And we won our share of those games.

We played basketball year round, interrupted occasionally by a softball game or track meet. In softball, the girls were an important part of our team. In fact, they were critical to our ability to field a team. There were some "big girls"—even sixth and seventh graders—who didn't play basketball but who were mainstays on the softball team because of their power at the plate. Track and field lost its appeal though, because most events were separated according to sex. Nina, the fleet-footed forward on the Walnut Grove basketball team, could have competed with the boys in any track event. We always wished she could have that chance.

As a high school student in the early 1950's, I saw the end of the one-room country school in Illinois. The country schools were consolidated one by one and then in groups until none remained. I visit now and drive by

Walnut Grove, but only a crumbling shell of the building stands. Some day I'll go back in the brush and weeds, and I'm sure I'll find the level place that used to be the basketball court. Perhaps a goal will still be standing.

I don't know where all those old teammates are now, boys or girls. Joan lives in California, Nina is still in southern Illinois, and Marilyn . . . I lost track of Marilyn a few years ago.

A solid "klunk" of the aluminum bat snapped me back to reality. I saw the ball dropping just beyond the reach of the second baseman. I saw my son dashing for third. The right fielder fumbled the ball, and the third-base coach waved my son home.

The game was over. Three boys' baseball teams had won this night in Huntsville, Texas, and three had lost. A team of girls had won a softball game; a team had lost. It was the first win of the season for the Oilers, and my son had scored the winning run. I felt good about that, but in the back of my mind something still didn't seem quite right . . . Nina would have gotten that ball over second base.

Street Games

Skelly

Skelly is a game with any number of players, and it can be played on a patio, in a driveway, or in the street.

With a piece of chalk draw the pattern for the playing field. See the diagram below. The outer edge should form a square about six feet by six feet. The smaller, numbered squares should be about one foot by one foot.

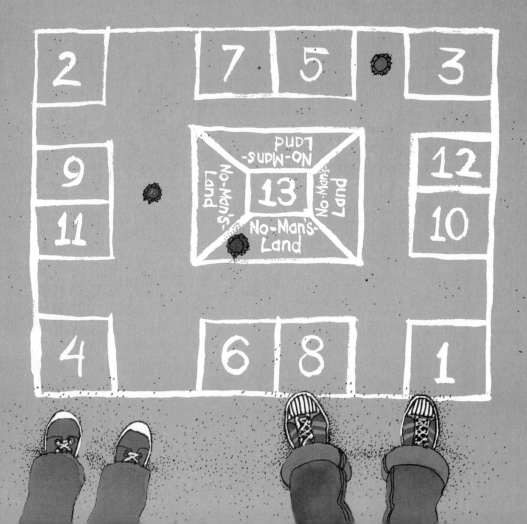

Candle Wax or Clay

A Bottle Cap

Next you need a bottle cap filled with candle wax, clay, or anything that will give it weight. To make the bottle cap go faster, you can rub it on the pavement until you have scraped off the writing and are down to the silver metal. When the bottle cap has this bare-metal look, it can glide along the street as if it were on ice.

The first player puts the shooter (bottle cap) on a line about twenty feet away and shoots for Box 1. Players keep shooting as long as they can get from one number to the next in a single shot (on the line doesn't count) or can hit another player's shooter. Players who land in No-Man's-Land are in real trouble. They have to stay there until they can talk a friend into knocking them out of it, and if they can't convince someone to do so, they must just stay around and continue to plead their case.

Players who get to Box 12 have two choices. The real heroes can shoot straight for Box 13 with, of course, a better-than-even chance of winding up in No-Man's-Land. The cautious kids can "go up the line"; that is, they can knock the shooter up one of the four lines running through the No-Man's-Land to Box 13. It is a slower way of getting there because they can move only three or four inches on each turn, but it is also a safer way because as long as the shooter is touching a line, it is out of No-Man's-Land. The player who gets to Box 13 first wins the game.

Flipping

This is a game for two players. You will need a collection of cards—the kind with pictures of baseball, football, basketball, or hockey players. These are usually sold in a package with a piece of bubble gum.

Flipping is a very simple operation, but it is an art, a game of skill. Each card has a head and a tail. The head is the side with the picture. The tail is the side that usually describes the picture.

First, decide how many cards to flip. Each person flips the card in basically the same way. Hold the card with the forefinger of the hand on one side of the card and the thumb on the other side of the card. With a gently swinging motion of the arm, card in hand, bring your arm down and back as if you were going to bowl. As your arm comes forward, release the card by snapping your wrist. If you are the first person to flip, and you decide on three cards, and your cards land on the sidewalk, two heads and a tail, your opponent has to match exactly—two heads and a tail. If the opponent does so, he or she wins the three cards you have flipped. If not, he or she loses.

Tug of War

No one is quite sure
how to win at Tug of War
except that you pull
and pullll   and pullllllll
and just as you're sure
you are winning,
the other team pulls
and pulllls   and pulllllllls
and you fall their way
and then they fall your way
but
if everyone on your team
should suddenly take a big breath
and tug all together
with arms around each other
then you might just possibly win.

Kathleen Fraser

The Toys

by Alice Ritchie

Len-Lu was a sailor's daughter. She lived with her mother in an old house on the waterside of a Chinese town, and when her father's ship was in port, he lived there, too. They were not rich, but Len-Lu had a very good time for all that. Her aunt and uncle kept a shop quite close to her mother's house, where they sold china and jade and silk embroideries, and as they had no children, they were particularly fond of Len-Lu, who went to see them nearly every day.

She helped them to set out the jade and ivory carvings on lacquer trays, and pretended to take a share in polishing the silver and copper bells of which they had a great number, but she was not expected to do any real work, because she was only nine years old. It was only a game to her, and as soon as she grew tired of it, she would wander off and play by herself among the tea chests and golden dragons in the upstairs rooms. Her uncle and aunt allowed her to go wherever she liked because they knew she would not break or spoil anything. "She has the neatest fingers in the world," they said.

So Len-Lu played at shops and at houses, but best of all she liked to play she was a sailor like her father, traveling to distant countries. She took a bamboo basket that was big enough for her to sit in and packed it with a set of ivory draughtsmen and painted fans and little figures made of jade and then got in carefully herself, and waved good-bye to the people on the shore and settled down for the long journey with her hands buried in

the sleeves of her coat—for she was the captain and did not have to do any work. But the ship sailed on and on, past the green lotus carvings, through the narrow passage between the big figures of wooden gods, into the clear space of polished floor near the door, where it stopped and she got out and walked about on foreign land. (Really she worked the basket over the slippery floor by pushing with her feet, but she pulled her long coat down so that they hardly showed, and pretended it was done by sailors.) She walked about on foreign land and sold her fans and draughtsmen and then got back into the empty ship and came quickly home with all flags flying and a bundle of money (it was really a lump of ivory tied up in an old scarf) to show to the people who were waiting on the pier beyond the lotus carvings.

That was her favorite game, but sometimes she grew tired of always pretending and then she would stand at the window and look out at the sea and all the real ships in the harbor. There were square-sailed fishing boats, and big junks, like the one her father sailed in, with high

prows and gilded figureheads, and English ships and French ships and Japanese ships, all flying their flags, some being loaded, some being unloaded, some coming in from long voyages, and some just disappearing away out to sea again. And she would stand there for a long time, wishing she could see her father's ship which had broad brown sails with scarlet dragons on them, and wishing that she, too, could put out to sea. So eagerly she watched that her uncle and aunt would call and call before she heard them and came down to her meal of fish and little brightly colored rice cakes and tea out of a doll's cup.

And then, one day, sure enough, she saw the ship with the scarlet dragons come sailing between the green headlands into the bay. She did not jump about and wave her arms and shout, because little Chinese girls never show their feelings in those ways, but she went straight downstairs and said to her uncle and aunt: "My father's ship has come in," and began to put on the wooden clogs she wore on her bare feet for walking in the streets.

"There is no hurry," said her uncle, smiling at her. "It will be hours before they have finished unloading and can come ashore."

"I shall tell Mother, and we'll go down to the pier and watch them," said Len-Lu. For all her quiet ways, her dark almond-shaped eyes were sparkling with joy.

She said good-bye to her uncle and aunt and found her mother, who was doing the washing in the courtyard behind her house, and told her the news, and they went off together to the pier. A good many other people were there already, but they managed to work their way to the front and watched her father's ship being unloaded. After a little while, they caught sight of him, and Len-Lu waved, and presently he saw her and waved back, but he had to turn away at once because they were very busy. Then Len-Lu's mother said she must go back to the house to prepare a grand welcome-home meal for her husband, and Len-Lu had to go, too, often turning to look back over her shoulder.

That evening they had a lovely time. Her uncle and aunt came in, and when her father had eaten and listened to all the news of home, he began to tell about the adventures of the voyage and the foreign lands he had visited. Len-Lu sat on her cushion beside him with her feet tucked under her and listened and listened without saying a word.

"Len-Lu would like to be a sailor, too, I believe," said her uncle, giving her a candied fig.

"Well," said her father, "it's a good life."

"I should not like to have two sailors in the family," said her mother. "For that reason, I am glad Len-Lu is a girl."

Len-Lu ate her fig and said nothing, but she thought a great many things which she kept to herself.

The next day her father took her down to the ship with him and let her walk about on the deck while he paid the sailors and saw that things were made ready for the next voyage. He was the next in rank to the captain, and so he had a great deal to do.

Len-Lu leaned against the deck rail and peeped through the holes in the carving—she was not tall enough to see over it—at the ship that lay next to them in the harbor. It was a big three-decker, all painted white, and flying a French flag. A band was playing on board and tall, pale-faced men in white clothes went quickly back and forth over the wide decks. To Len-Lu the ship seemed like a piece of the foreign lands she longed so much to see, and she stared and stared at it until it was time to go home with her father.

"When will you have a ship of your own?" she asked as they walked to their house.

"As soon as I possibly can save enough money," said her father. He wanted more than anything in the world to be captain of a ship of his own.

A few days after this, Len-Lu fell ill—not very ill, but ill enough to have to stay indoors all day. She could not even go to her uncle's shop, but when she was getting better he came to see her, and to help her to pass the dull time, he taught her to make paper toys. He used the crinkly kind of paper that people in England decorate their rooms with at Christmas time, but he made all sorts of things out of it—pagodas and dragons and flowers, and he fixed them each on two thin sticks to hold them by, and so cunningly that by just giving them a shake the pagodas changed their color from orange to pink, or white to green, the dragons lashed their tails, and the flowers opened out from small buds into chrysanthemums as big as his hand, and then, at another shake, they went back again as they were at first.

Len-Lu was soon able to make them, too, because she was so neat and quick with her fingers. But all the same she was glad when she was able to get up and go to the ship again with her father.

The time for the next voyage was drawing near. The sailors were busy all day now, the hold was filled with the cargo, the sails were mended and ready; Len-Lu's mother finished the new pair of trousers she was making for her husband and at last the time came when he had to go. He said good-bye to Len-Lu in the house, but he did not notice that she slipped out of the room immediately afterwards and went into the courtyard where his luggage was waiting to be carried to the ship. It was in two big bamboo baskets, tied on either end of a bamboo pole which he would carry across his shoulder.

Len-Lu lifted the canvas covering of the baskets and saw that they were not full right up to the top. She quickly took some of the things out of one and put them in the other until it was nearly full, drew the cover over it neatly, and then went back to the first basket which now had only a few soft clothes at the bottom, and jumped in and curled herself up as she used to do when she played at being a sailor in the basket at her uncle's house, and pulled the canvas cover over her head.

Presently her father came out of the house; he raised the pole and put it across his shoulder, and she heard him give a little surprised grunt when he found it heavier than he had expected. However, he did not imagine that anything was wrong with it, and he set off to the ship without an idea that he was taking his daughter with him. The baskets joggled up and down on the ends of the springy bamboo, and it was quite dark for Len-Lu under the canvas cover; she folded her hands together under the sleeves of her coat, just as she always did when she was playing her game, but now she did not need to work with her feet in order to move her ship. She sat quite still. They went along the narrow street and then took the sharp turn to the left for the jetty. A little boat was waiting there to take her father to his ship. He climbed in and set the baskets down carefully beside him, but when they came to the big ship there was a rather anxious moment for Len-Lu, because, as no one knew there was anything except clothes and other belongings in the basket, the sailors were not particularly careful as to how they held it when they were getting it up the steep side of the ship. She did not know for a moment whether she was right side up or not, or in which direction the sky was and which the sea. But she sat quite still and kept her hands folded, and, luckily for her, her father called to the sailors to be careful, as the covers were not sewn on the baskets and he did not want to see his clothes fall into the harbor. He little knew that his daughter might have fallen in there, too.

They carried the baskets into his cabin and set them down and everyone went away to take a share in getting the ship out to sea. Len-Lu sat quietly with the canvas cover still over her head. She did not dare to stir until she felt the ship moving, in case they sent her home again. She heard the captain and her father shouting and the sailors singing as they pulled on the ropes, and at last she felt the ship bound forward under a fair wind, all sails set for a foreign land.

She pushed back the canvas cover and crept out, blinking in the sudden light, but calm and composed as ever, and when her father came in some time later he got the greatest shock he had ever had, for a voice said "Father!" and, looking up, he saw his daughter standing there in her black coat with her hands clasped in front of her. At first he thought something terrible must have happened to her or to his wife, and that she was a vision, come to tell him of it, but when she smiled and held out her hands he knew she was real, and when he noticed the thrown-back cover of the bamboo basket, he understood what she had done and knew that he had his daughter with him at sea.

What to do about it he did not know. The ship could not put back now or they would lose the good wind that was taking them so quickly over the first stages of their voyage; nor would scolding her be very useful. So he decided to take her to the captain to ask for his orders, and they went off hand in hand. The captain looked very surprised when he saw a little girl on his ship and he frowned in a frightening way when her father told him the story, but at the end of it he suddenly began to laugh.

"So you wanted to be a sailor!" he said, turning his long black mustache on Len-Lu. "Well, since you came with us, you must stay with us. But do not forget that you must be good and quiet."

Len-Lu nodded; it was not difficult for her to promise that, because she always was good and quiet.

"So that is settled," said her father when they were alone again, "but all the same, you do not seem to have considered other people's feelings as you

185

should. What do you suppose your mother and your kind uncle and aunt are thinking now? They believe you are lost, and probably drowned."

"No," said Len-Lu, and she explained that she had left a message that her uncle, who was used to her way of telling him things, for she could not write, would understand and explain to the others. She had set her bamboo boat in the middle of the lumber room where she played, and in it she had laid a piece of paper cut out and colored like the French flag, and a button from her father's coat and a scrap of her own hair screwed up in a twist of stuff from an old jacket. The button stood for her father, the hair for herself, and the French flag for foreign lands, and her uncle would know that the message meant, "We have gone on a voyage together."

"He will be a clever man if he guesses that," said her father, but Len-Lu insisted that he would read her meaning at once.

And then the lovely days began for Len-Lu. They had the most wonderful weather on that voyage; the good wind stayed with them, the sun shone over the blue sea, the ship sailed through the narrow passages between the white islands where terrible storms have usually to be faced, without encountering anything more frightening than flying fish and dolphins. The sailors said Len-Lu had brought them good luck, and even the captain said once that if she could not pull her weight upon a rope at least she had done something to pay for her passage in arranging the weather so nicely. They were all fond of her, and she helped them in whatever ways she could, such as mending their clothes, for she sewed very neatly. They told her stories and let her go wherever she liked on the ship. She would stand for hours staring through

the holes in the carving of the deck rail at the blue sea, flecked with white waves that never broke; sometimes she saw another Chinese junk and sometimes a foreign ship, and every now and then they passed near enough to the shore for her to see strange houses and trees, looking tiny because of the distance. In the evenings she sat beside her father under the lantern in their sleeping place, and while he smoked and dreamed about the days when he would be a captain, she passed the time by making dragons and pagodas and chrysanthemums out of crinkly paper that a sailor had given her, in the way her uncle had taught her when she was ill. And, later, when the lantern was put out, she would lie in her little bunk and listen to the sea making a sleepy sound on the other side of the wooden wall, and wish it was morning so that she could run quickly up on deck again.

Day after day went by like this, but at last they sighted land. Len-Lu stood beside the sailors on the deck, and they all watched the green hills and the white houses

draw nearer and nearer to them—it seemed as if it was the land and not the ship that was moving. Lee-Song, a special friend of Len-Lu's, who had made this voyage many times, stood near her, and when they had drawn still closer, he pointed out the different buildings in the great town and told her what they were.

"Would you like to come ashore with me?" he asked. "I shall be free to go before your father is." Len-Lu said she would like it very much if her father gave his permission.

"I was thinking," went on Lee-Song, who was a clever man and knew that the common things in one country are rare in another, "that it would be a good thing if you took with you the paper toys you have been making on the voyage to sell to the people in the town. They have never seen anything like your dragons and pagodas."

Len-Lu shook her head; she was too shy, she did not believe her toys were good enough to sell to anybody.

"Just as you like," said Lee-Song. "I am going to take my carvings"—he did very clever wood carvings when it was not his turn for duty at sea—"and I shall come back to the ship with a lot of money in my handkerchief. But do just as you like, so far as your toys are concerned."

Len-Lu remembered the ivory ball she used to tie up in a scarf and play was the money she had made, in her games in her uncle's warehouse, and she thought how splendid it would be and how like a real sailor and not just a passenger to come back to her ship with money in a handkerchief. So, although she still felt very shy, she nodded her head this time instead of shaking it.

"That is right," said Lee-Song.

He brought a flat bamboo basket with a lid and they went below to her father's sleeping place and packed it with the paper toys and fastened the lid carefully over them and Lee-Song took charge of it. Len-Lu hoped he would not tell any of the other sailors what she was going to do, but she was too shy to ask him not to, and went away and stood beside her father while the ship moved slowly to its place against the wharf. The brown sails with the red dragons were furled; the flag flew at the masthead. On the shore people said to each other, "Oh, do look at that curious ship! What is it?" And the ones who knew said, "It is a Chinese trading junk." The ship had come safely to France.

The captain shouted his order, and sailors ran quickly over the decks; everyone was in a bustle and fuss. But presently Lee-Song came to Len-Lu's side.

"I am allowed to go ashore now," he said. "Are you coming?"

Len-Lu looked up at her father and when he nodded to her, too busy to take much notice, she went off with Lee-Song.

They climbed down the ladder onto the wharf and went up the busy street that led into the center of the town. It was a fine day and a great many people were about. Len-Lu stared and stared with all her eyes at the strange faces and the strange clothes. Even the buildings were strange to her, and the noises, and the very smells were different from the ones she was used to in her own country. She held on to the edge of Lee-Song's blue

tunic with one hand for fear she would lose the last familiar thing she had. When a tram came around the corner suddenly, she almost forgot about never showing her feelings, and did in fact give one little gasp, because just for a second she thought it was a live dragon with people sitting in its inside. It was almost too exciting. But Lee-Song marched cheerfully along, knowing the place well, and enjoying being on shore again. He halted when he came to a place where people were sitting at small round tables eating and drinking out in the street. It was a fashionable restaurant, and it was just about twelve o'clock. Most of the tables were occupied.

"Now!" he said, smiling at Len-Lu, opening the basket of toys and setting it at her feet. "Here is a good place for you to stand. Take some of the toys in your hands and show how they work. I shall go over to the other side of the tables, not far away, with my carvings. And, Len-Lu, when they ask you how much there is to pay, you must hold up one finger, like this." (In that way everyone would know that they had to pay one franc each for a toy.)

Lee-Song went over to the other side of the tables and unwrapped his carvings. Len-Lu picked up a dragon, holding the two sticks in her hands to make him lash his tail and shake his head back and forth. She was very shy and rather frightened as well, but she did not show any of her feelings in her face.

Soon the people sitting at the nearest table saw her. "Why, look! There's a Chinese baby!" they said. "Isn't she sweet?" They thought Len-Lu was younger than she was because she was so small. "What has she got in her

hand?" asked the little boy at the table. "Oh, look! Oh, look!" For Len-Lu now took up a chrysanthemum branch and shook the buds out into flowers and back again into buds. The little boy screamed with delight.

"Is she selling them?" asked his mother.

"I'll ask her," said his father, and he got up and came across to Len-Lu.

He looked very big and terrifying, striding towards her, the white-faced foreign man, but she did not budge, and when he said, in French, because he could not speak Chinese: "Are you selling these pretty things, my child?" she held up her finger as Lee-Song had told her, hoping that would be a right answer to whatever he had said.

"One franc!" he said. "Come over here, Etienne, and choose which you want!"

The little boy came up eagerly, and his father not only bought him whatever he asked for but he chose a pagoda for himself and a chrysanthemum branch for his wife, and when he went back to his table they both played with them, making the pagoda change color and the chrysanthemums open and shut, and enjoying it as if they were children themselves.

Soon the people at the other tables noticed them. What is it? Where did they get those things? Can't we have one? they asked each other, and then they saw Len-Lu with her basket, and immediately someone came from every table to buy for the rest, they were all so eager to have one of the pretty toys to play with as they sat in the sun listening to the band and eating their lunch. Lee-Song had to come over to help her, it all went so fast, and the money was hard for her to handle. "Dear little thing!" the foreign people said—there were English and Americans there as well as French—"Oh, really she is a darling!" and although Len-Lu did not understand their language, she knew they were all friendly and liked her toys, and she enjoyed herself enormously as she handed out dragons and pagodas and chrysanthemums and showed them how they ought to be shaken, and smiled and smiled.

At last the basket was quite empty and Lee-Song's carvings were all sold.

"We must go back to the ship," he said, but first he put Len-Lu's money in a handkerchief and tied it with a hard knot and gave it to her to carry. "Hold it tight," he said. He need not have worried, because she was far too proud and happy to run any risk of losing it.

"Would you like to use some of your money to ride back to the ship in one of those things?" he asked, pointing to a tram, but Len-Lu shook her head. She wanted her father to untie the knot in the handkerchief himself and see all the money she had made for him—every penny of it.

He was even more surprised and pleased when he saw it than she could have hoped.

"This means more than you think," he said, getting up and walking back and forth in his excitement. "It has given me a good idea. Len-Lu, would you like to come with me on all my voyages?"

"I think you know that I have always wanted to go to sea," said Len-Lu.

"I guessed it when I knew you had come aboard in my clothes basket!" said her father.

"And I like it even better than I thought I would," she said.

"Well, then, listen, Len-Lu," said her father. "When we get home, I shall sell our house and with that money and what we shall save by not having any housekeeping on shore, I shall be able to afford to buy a ship, and your mother and you will come with me on all my voyages, and when we are in China we shall stay with your uncle and aunt. Thus I shall be a captain long before I expected, and you will pay for your passage by making these toys and selling them in the foreign lands we visit. Len-Lu," he added tenderly, "you have made your family's fortune." And that is exactly what happened.

Create a Party Mask

Len-Lu not only made flowers and toys, she also made paper masks for people to wear at parties. The mask shown here was one of her favorites. You can be as clever as Len-Lu if you follow the directions on these pages.

Get a piece of lightweight paper, a large piece of heavy paper, scissors, a pencil, cord or ribbon, and colored pencils, pens, or paints.

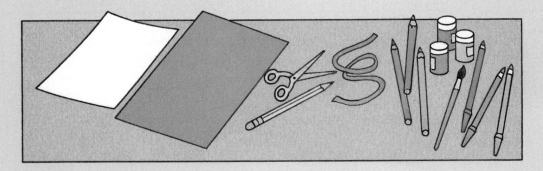

Do this:
- Make a pattern, using the basic mask pattern on page 197. Add your own ideas to the basic pattern and cut it out.
- Fold the piece of heavy paper in half. On the paper trace around your mask pattern. Be sure to draw the straight edge of the pattern on the fold of the paper.
- Cut out the drawn pattern, keeping the paper folded.

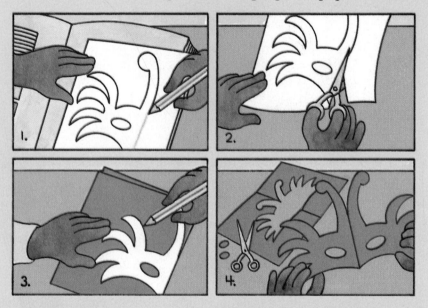

- Unfold the paper and you will see the whole mask.
- Decorate the mask, using colored pencils, pens, or paints.
- Make a small hole on each side of the mask.
- Knot the cord or ribbon through each hole.
- Tie the cord or ribbon in back to hold the mask in place.

Create original mask patterns to use in plays or to wear at parties.

Basic Mask Pattern

The Batboy Who Played

by Furman Bisher

The year was 1952. Everywhere the Fitzgerald team of the Georgia State League went, Joe Reliford went along. Joe was batboy and general handyboy. He was good-sized for a boy of twelve, almost big enough to be a member of the team. Sometimes the players let him sneak into the batting cage and get a few swings before a game. Joe could swing a bat well.

The players liked Joe because he was fun loving. And Joe liked the players because they were good to him and made him feel like one of them. For a lad in a small town, being batboy is an important position. Everybody in Fitzgerald, and in several other towns in the league, knew Joe Reliford.

Joe's favorite player was the Fitzgerald second base-man, Charlie Ridgeway. Charlie would often sit beside Joe on the bus coming home from a game in another town. And Charlie would talk baseball with Joe. This made Joe feel grown-up.

Joe liked speed in a baseball player, and Ridgeway was the fastest runner in the Georgia State League. One season Ridgeway had stolen over sixty bases, and Joe was sure that he would someday see his hero play in the big leagues. Charlie never made the big leagues, but before the end of the season, he got a better job.

One day the president and manager of the Fitzgerald team, Ace Adams, called Ridgeway into the clubhouse and said, "Charlie, I've got a surprise for you. You're the new manager."

Adams had been managing the team and also trying to handle the business matters. The work was too much for him, so he made Ridgeway his manager on the field.

Ridgeway had been the manager for a week when the Fitzgerald team was supposed to play the Statesboro team. The Statesboro Elks Club was having a special "night" for the home team. A big crowd turned out for the game.

The sight of a filled park seemed to make the Statesboro players want to play their best. They got one base hit after another off Fitzgerald. And Joe Reliford looked on sadly as Charlie Ridgeway's new job took a bad turn. The score became so one-sided that the crowd began teasing Joe.

By the eighth inning, Statesboro was leading by the score of 13–0. The fans began shouting the ballpark cry, "Put in the batboy! Put in the batboy!"

By this time, Ridgeway was willing to do anything. "Why not put in the batboy? If the crowd wants a show, we'll give 'em a show," Ridgeway said to himself.

Ridgeway called time and held a quick meeting with the umpire, a young man named Eddie Kubick. "They're yelling for the batboy, Eddie," Ridgeway said. "Our batboy's got on a uniform, and he swings a pretty good bat. I've seen him in practice. What's wrong with putting him in the game?"

"Nothing, as far as I know," Kubick said. "But even if you score more runs, you'll lose because you're using a player who is not on the team."

"The way things are going," Ridgeway said, "that isn't likely to happen. Reliford batting for Nichting."

Ridgeway went back to the dugout and told Joe to get a bat. He told Nichting, the leading hitter on the team, to be seated.

"You're joking, aren't you, Mr. Charlie?" Joe asked.

"They've been yelling for a batboy," Ridgeway said, "we'll give 'em the batboy. Get a stick and get up there."

Joe waited a moment. Then he grabbed a bat and walked up to the plate. The crowd howled. Curtis White, the Statesboro pitcher, shook his head and looked at Kubick. The umpire called for the pitch as the announcement was made to the crowd over the public address system:

"Reliford batting for Nichting."

The crowd howled louder. Joe scratched the dirt with his shoe and waved the bat. White had a two-hitter going at the time, and he was taking no chances. He cut

loose with a good fastball. Joe swung and smashed the
ball toward the third baseman. It looked like a base hit,
but the third baseman made a good catch and threw Joe
out at first base by a step. But Joe had tried hard, and
the crowd now cheered him.

Ridgeway went all the way with his batboy. He threw him Nichting's glove and sent him to right field. One of the Statesboro players, Charlie Quimby, had a hit in each of the last twenty-one games. But tonight he was hitless when he came to bat for the last time in the eighth inning. He sent a sinking line drive to right field that looked like a sure hit. Joe ran for the ball. Just when it looked as though he would never make it, he stuck out his glove and made a beautiful catch. Ray Nichting could never have made the catch. Not only was Ray a slow runner, but he led the league in errors by outfielders that season.

The Statesboro crowd stood and cheered the batboy as he ran in from the outfield with a broad grin on his face. Joe never got a chance to go to bat again because the Fitzgerald team went down in order in the ninth inning.

It would have been a sad ride back to Fitzgerald that night but for the subject of Joe Reliford. The players, seemingly trying to forget their loss, carried on loudly and proudly about his part in the game.

"Better sign him up, Skipper," one said to Ridgeway, "before he gets away."

Ridgeway raised his voice above the noise on the bus. "Fellows," he said, "if you never make it to the big leagues, you can always say you've done something no big leaguer has ever done. You've played with the youngest fellow that ever played baseball in our league."

He put his arm around Joe Reliford and gave him a big wink.

What's Your Batting Average?

Joe Reliford, the batboy, almost made a hit in a baseball game. How many hits can you make?

To make a hit, start at home plate. Read the group of words near that base. Think of one prefix that can be added to each word in the group to make a new word. Write the new words on a piece of paper.

For example,

___ load   unload

___ tie   untie

\+   un   =

___ certain   uncertain

___ comfortable   uncomfortable

Count one point for each hit you make.

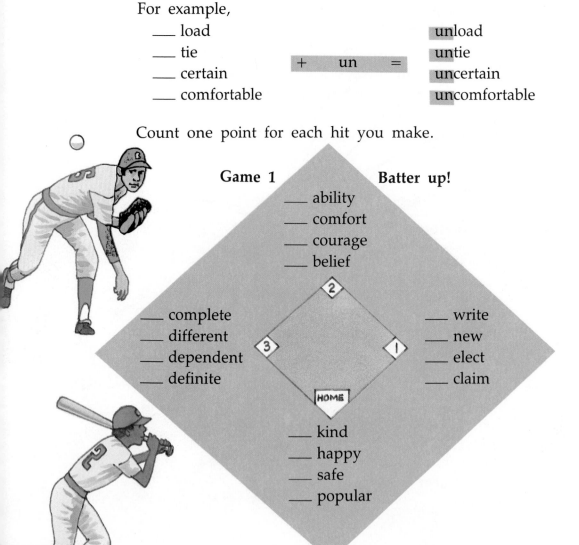

Game 1   **Batter up!**

___ ability
___ comfort
___ courage
___ belief

___ complete   ___ write
___ different   ___ new
___ dependent   ___ elect
___ definite   ___ claim

HOME

___ kind
___ happy
___ safe
___ popular

In Game 2 you must think of one suffix that can be added to each word in the group to make a new word. Write the new words on your paper.

For example,

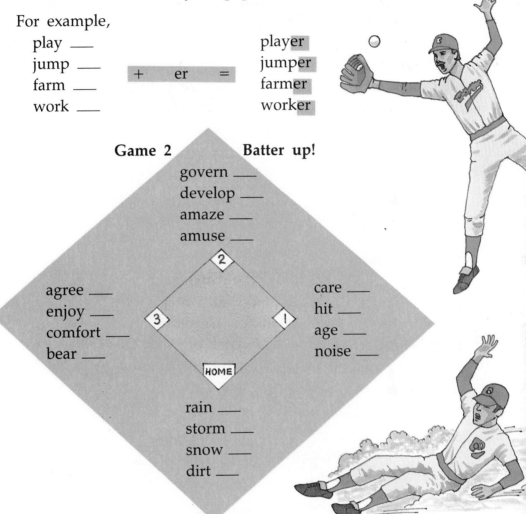

play ——   player

jump ——   +   er   =   jumper

farm ——   farmer

work ——   worker

Game 2   **Batter up!**

govern ——
develop ——
amaze ——
amuse ——

agree ——   care ——
enjoy ——   hit ——
comfort ——   age ——
bear ——   noise ——

rain ——
storm ——
snow ——
dirt ——

If anyone challenges a word you have made, you must prove it is a real word by finding it in a dictionary. What's your batting average?

Use some of the words you made to write a story about your favorite sport.

The Game of Seven Tans

Can you imagine making over 1,600 pictures by using one square cut into seven pieces?

For over 200 years people have been enjoying the game known as Tangrams. They have challenged their imagination by creating pictures of animals, plants, people, and objects from these puzzle pieces.

No one knows for certain where the game began. Some say that the name *tangrams* comes from the Chinese riverboat *Tanka* girls who taught the game to foreign sailors. Others say that the game took its name from the English word *trangram*, meaning "toy" or "trinket." They think that Dr. Johnson spelled the word wrong in his dictionary.

A Chinese book published in 1803 tells about this game. By 1818 books and magazines spread the news about tangrams in the United States, Germany, France, and England. The writer of *Alice in Wonderland*, Lewis Carroll, and a great poet, Edgar Allan Poe, were known to have played the game.

How to Make the Game

You will need:

a piece of cardboard 6 inches square,
sharp scissors, a pencil, and a ruler

Then do this:

1. Mark off the 6-inch square into 16 small squares. Make each square 1½ inches. Use your ruler carefully and make light pencil lines.

206

2. Letter the entire square like the pattern below.
3. Make heavier lines connecting *E* with *K*, and point *A* with *DH*.
4. Connect point *J* with *G*, and point *G* with *DF*.
5. Draw a line between points *DH* and *BH*.
6. Cut along the heavy lines very carefully. You should have seven small pieces, or tans—two large triangles, one middle-sized triangle, two small triangles, one square, and one rhomboid.

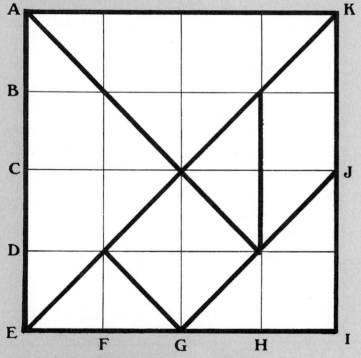

How to Play the Game

Use your imagination and think of an animal, a plant, a person, or an object that you wish to create by using your tans. Then arrange the seven tans to form the object. All seven tans must be used in each picture that you create. See how many designs or figures you can make.

Did You Know?

According to carvings found on ancient tombs, the Egyptians played board games as early as 2500 B.C.

Some of the favorite games played by children in ancient Rome were bowling hoops, blindman's buff, and tug-of-war.

Children living during the Middle Ages in Europe played with puppets and rattles.

Ball games were being played by Indians in Central America long before Christopher Columbus sailed to the New World.

The first toy balloons were made of paper in China hundreds of years ago. Rubber balloons were not made until the 1800's.

Children in colonial America enjoyed playing the games hopscotch, leapfrog, London Bridge, and hide-and-seek. They also played with balls, dolls, marbles, tops, kites, jump ropes, and rolling hoops.

208

Books for You

Street Games by Alan Milberg

Learn the origins of many street games, the materials needed to play, the directions for playing, and variations of the games.

The Indian in the Cupboard by Lynn Reid Banks

The toy Indian that Omri received for his birthday isn't very exciting compared to the mysterious cupboard and its key. But the Indian, Little Bear, comes to life when placed in the cupboard, and Omri must make some difficult decisions.

The Dollhouse Caper by Jean S. O'Connell

Three boys who own a dollhouse are alerted by the dollhouse family to the danger of a robbery.

The Egypt Game by Zilpha Keatley Snyder

Two girls develop a common interest in ancient Egypt and begin to develop a "land of Egypt" in an abandoned storage yard.

The Great American Book of Sidewalk, Stoop, Dirt, Curb, and Alley Games by Fred Ferretti

Here is a handbook of more than sixty American street games. Also included are the variations of names and rules for each game.

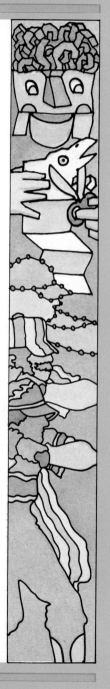

A Pot of Water for Bokkas

by Winnie Wyatt

A hot, dry wind tickled Bokkas's knees as he crouched between the twisted roots of a big flame tree. He was watching his two little brothers chase each other around the tree's scaly trunk. On the wave of the wind came his mother's voice. "Bokkas! Go to the watering place and see if the pot is filled."

The slender African boy rose reluctantly to his task, tripping one of his little brothers as the child sped around the tree. Bokkas helped him to his feet, scolding, "There! Watch where you are going! It is because you cannot stand on your feet that I am called to do your work again." Actually, Bokkas was too big to be carrying water, for he was now allowed to sit outside the men's circle at night and listen to their talk. Carrying water was the task of the two little brothers. However, last week, while playing along the trail, one of them stumbled and spilled his pot of water. So now Bokkas had to carry all the water, for water was too precious to be wasted.

"Bokkas!" His mother's voice was more urgent this time.

"I am just going, Mother," he called.

Under the shadow of her hut's wide, low grass eaves, where she sat shelling corn, his mother smiled at her son's departing back. How tall her first-born had grown!

The dust of the much-used trail to the water hole was hot and powdery between Bokkas's bare toes. The rains had stopped early, cutting short the growing season, and it would be many weeks before they returned. Not a blade of grass, nor even a weed, grew in the parched ground near the village. There was little shade from the few trees. The grass roofs on the mud-walled houses were faded and gray under the hot sun.

Week by week the water hole had become more sluggish and was slower to send water through the little opening in the earth where someone had placed a piece of metal to direct its flow into a waiting water pot. Each day the pots were filled more and more slowly.

Last week the chief of the village had warned that all must be very careful in the use of water. Certain rules of conservation must be obeyed. No clothes were to be washed. This did not bother Bokkas, for he and his brothers wore little clothing in the dry season when it was hot. Next the chief had said there must be no bathing except for very small children. At this Bokkas was saddened, for he loved the feel of cool water trickling off his ears when his little brothers poured it from a dripping bucket onto his head. And today the chief had decreed that water must be used only for cooking and drinking; even the babies must go unwashed.

The earth around the water hole was moist, but Bokkas viewed his mother's water pot with concern. Since he had placed it here two hours ago scarcely a cup of water had dripped into it, and there were several other empty pots waiting to be filled. What would his village do? Would they starve for both food and water? Many of the women had only millet softened in water and then boiled to feed their families. Soon there would not even be water for soaking the tiny, round grains.

Bokkas dug his hot toes into the damp earth around the pot. Suddenly, the feel of the moist dirt under his toes reminded him of something he had almost forgotten. Not long ago he had been gathering sticks on the other side of the hill for his mother's cooking fire. He had stopped to rest in a place sheltered by high elephant grass where the ground under his feet had felt cool and wet, just as it did here. At the time, he had not thought of anything except how pleasant the coolness had been to the rough soles of his feet. But now a thought came to Bokkas. Perhaps there might be water hiding in an underground stream in that spot just as there had been here, before the villagers dug the earth away and directed the water's flow into their water pots.

Bokkas hardly felt the scratching, dry brush against his bare legs as he left the trail and skirted the hillside in search of the place. Finding the exact spot under the hill proved more of a problem than he had thought, for there were no paths on that side of the low mountain, and every clump of grass looked the same. His feet were the first to tell him that he was close, for the earth was becoming cooler. Using his feet as guides, he moved in a circle to the spot that seemed most moist. Then kneeling, he began scratching away at the sand and grass around it. Gradually the sand became wetter until Bokkas, up to his elbows in the hole he had dug with his bare hands,

could almost feel the flow of sand and water through his fingers. Excitedly he refilled the hole with the sand he had taken away so that none of the precious drops of water could escape and spill down the hillside.

Bokkas did not stop at his mother's house, but ran straight to the compound of the chief and threw himself before the village ruler. Even without permission, the young boy began to speak. "Oh, chief! I have found water! I have found water for our village. There is water ready to fill our pots!"

"What does the child say?" the old man asked those who stood near him.

"He says he has found water," they answered.

So great was his excitement, the chief spoke directly to the child still lying before him. "Are you sure, child? The wisest ones from our village have looked in vain for water holes, and even the trusted springs have become dry."

Bokkas raised himself so that he was crouched on hands and knees, his face lifted to the the village ruler. "I know I have found water, chief. It was even rushing through my fingers as I dug in the sand."

Bokkas led the way to his water hole. The chief, carried on the arms of his four bodyguards, followed with all the village behind. Bokkas wanted to run and dance with excitement but held himself straight and dignified as he marched in front of the chief's litter. Once he looked back and could not see the end of the long trail of people from his village, each with a pot for filling with water. In his heart Bokkas said a prayer that there might be enough water from his spring to fill all the containers.

Men of the village removed the sand from the spring with swift, powerful strokes. But it was Bokkas who was allowed to fill the first earthen pot with the cool water that bubbled up from the depths of the earth. As the pots were filled, the people formed a dancing line to return joyfully to the village. Bokkas, standing beside the water hole, watched them go. He did not understand how anyone could dance with a filled water pot on one's head and never spill a drop. He could carry great loads on his head, as he had been taught almost from the time that he could walk, but only those who had spent a lifetime carrying headloads could learn to dance under the weight of them.

There was dancing in the village until very late that night. Bokkas, almost a hero, was honored with a seat near the chief. Before the chief retired, he held up his hands for silence, and the drummers and dancers were quiet. "We have had good fortune today," he declared to them. "We have been led to cool water by the hand of a child.

"Even though we have found new water," the chief went on, "we still must be careful until the rains return. Use only small amounts for washing. Anyone judged to be wasteful will be forced to go without water for a day." The people nodded their agreement and acceptance of their ruler's wisdom.

The chief then turned to Bokkas, sitting at his feet. "Now, my child," he said, "because you have brought gladness to our village, we want to honor you. What do you wish as a gift—a handful of kola nuts for your very own or a new piece of cloth for a robe such as our men wear?"

Bokkas thought a moment, weighing the advantages of both gifts. Kola was very scarce, and only the rich in the village chewed the bitter nut. In the last weeks of dryness, only the chief and his council could afford this privilege, for the nut was brought by traders from the south. Bokkas could not even imagine the richness of a whole handful of white kola nuts for his very own. Then he thought of the cloth the chief had offered. He had never owned a robe such as men wore, for it required yards and yards of cloth and was too costly for the children. For a moment Bokkas pictured himself walking grandly around the village in his flowing robes with all the other boys looking at him. The boy enjoyed this mental picture just briefly, for he was soon to be a man and must not take lightly the gifts offered him by his chief.

Bokkas bowed respectfully before the old man as he spoke. "Good chief, the thing that I have done is too small for gifts. I would feel ashamed while chewing kola or wearing a robe to think that I must be honored for sharing the gift of water with my village."

The chief was silent for a moment, and all the drums

were still. "It is spoken well, my son. Is there nothing we could do to show you honor for what you have done?"

"There is one thing, my chief." Bok-kas smiled uncertainly. "If it is not judged too wasteful, might I have a pot of water all my own for pouring over my head and body?"

The chief laughed and clapped his leg with his leather fan. "It shall be done! A pot of water is a small thing for one who discovered its source."

Before he went to sleep, cool and refreshed from the shower of water his little brothers had poured over his head, Bokkas's mother slipped into the hut and sat on the earth floor beside him.

"I, too, have an honor for you, my son—you shall no more have to carry water from the water hole."

Bokkas protested, although it was not a chore he enjoyed. "But, Mother, the clumsy little boys will spill our precious water."

"They will learn. Carrying water is not work for you," she answered.

Bokkas again protested weakly. "But, Mother, I yet have several seasons left for growing taller."

Bokkas's mother pulled a sleeping cloth over her first-born to protect him against the chill of the dusty wind that would soon be blowing through the village. "Do not make argument with your mother, my son. It is for her to decide when you have grown tall."

Vocabulary Potpourri

Bokkas was very clever and liked to play word games with his friends in the village. One of the games was called Vocabulary Potpourri. First, he would think of a word. Using a small stick or twig, Bokkas would make as many horizontal lines in the sand as there are letters in the word. Then, he would give his friends a clue to the meaning of the word. His friends would try to guess the word.

Some word-meaning clues that Bokkas gave his friends follow. Copy the word-meaning clues and the exact number of lines on a piece of paper. Read each word meaning. Think of a word that has this meaning. To help you find the word, look on the page that is in parentheses. The lines tell you how many letters are in the word. Then write the word.

1. unwillingly (210) ◯ __ __ __ __ __ __ __ __ __ __

2. protection from being
   used up (211) __ __ __ __ ◯ __ __ __ __ __ __

3. wet; slightly damp (212) __ __ __ ◯ __

4. consent (213) __ __ __ __ __ __ __ __ ◯ __

5. using too much (216) __ __ __ __ __ __ ◯ __

6. strongly objected (217) __ ◯ __ __ __ __ __ __

7. head of a village (214) ◯ __ __ __ __

8. special favor;
   advantage (215) __ __ __ __ __ __ ◯ __ __

Look at your answers. In order, write the letter that is circled in each word. This will help you complete the sentence about water. Write the sentence on your paper.

Water is an important __ __ __ __ __ __ __ __ .
                                         1   2   3   4   5   6   7   8

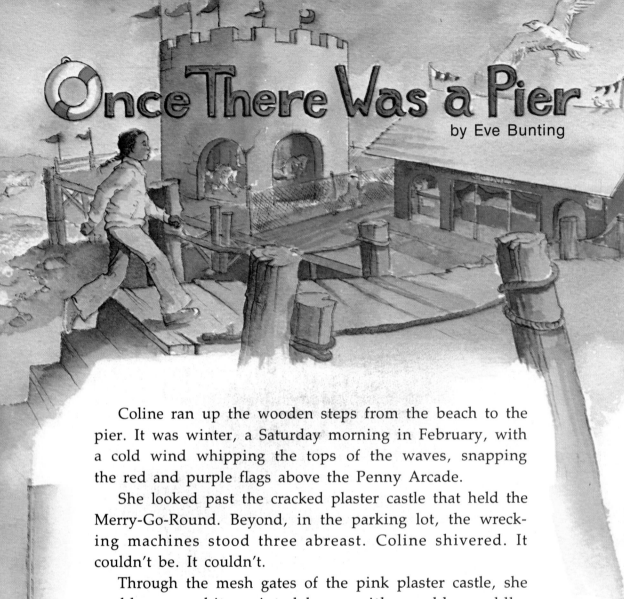

Once There Was a Pier

by Eve Bunting

Coline ran up the wooden steps from the beach to the pier. It was winter, a Saturday morning in February, with a cold wind whipping the tops of the waves, snapping the red and purple flags above the Penny Arcade.

She looked past the cracked plaster castle that held the Merry-Go-Round. Beyond, in the parking lot, the wrecking machines stood three abreast. Coline shivered. It couldn't be. It couldn't.

Through the mesh gates of the pink plaster castle, she could see a white painted horse with a golden saddle. Parnassus! The horse's neck was arched, the creamy mane seemed to blow in the wind, the teeth snapped at the bit. What if the wreckers came? Coline closed her eyes and turned quickly away.

The pier was early-morning empty. Far out, past the concession stands, two lone anglers leaned on the wooden railings.

Sam Wing was mopping the cement strip in front of the Sea Food Shanty. He wore rubber boots and a dark blue apron. Behind him large lobsters crawled in the bubbling tank, their spiky antennae rattling against the glass. Big red snappers lay head to tail; gritty shelled mussels and shrimps were frozen together in a square of white and coral. The air smelled of the bottom of the sea.

Coline jumped the swishing strands of Sam's mop. "What happened, Sam? What did the council decide?"

Sam Wing plunged his mop into the bucket of suds, slopping water over the edge. He shook his head without looking up.

"I don't believe it." Coline heard the shake in her own voice. "Didn't Mr. Esler speak up? And the congressman? They must have listened to the congressman."

"Not this congressman. We lost, Coline. The pier goes."

Coline made a circle in the wet sand with the toe of her sneaker. "Does Phil know?"

"I guess. I guess we all know."

Next door, Stella the Stargazer wiped the night's spray from the window of her little house. Her black hair was bunched into fat pink rollers.

Coline stopped. "Have you heard, Stella?"

Stella peeled a sticky label from the wooden sign that hung over her door. The sign said HELP WITH ALL YOUR PROBLEMS. The label said SAVE THE PIER. The label clung for a moment to the railing before it fluttered down into the water.

"There's no saving it now, hon," Stella said.

Coline jammed her hands into the pockets of her jeans. "How come you saw in your crystal ball that the pier would stay, Stella?" She was angry with Stella, with everyone.

"Wishful thinking, my friend. In my business I tell people what they want to hear. I tell me what I want to hear." She sighed and opened her door, and Coline saw the round table with the crystal ball, the vase of red plastic carnations, the framed picture of President Kennedy, who had died a long time ago.

She walked slowly on. Stella the Stargazer! Stella the Big Fake!

Here, beyond the breaking waves, the water was quiet. Two surfers in wet suits paddled their boards. The old seal lay on the fishing float, its coat as black and slick as the rubber tires that circled the raft. There was the smell of fish and rope and stale popcorn. Her feet made the loose boards rattle, and she stopped to look through at the sea swelling below. Weeds drifted like mermaid hair, green and tangled. The old wood groaned and creaked with every movement of the ocean. Unsafe. No way to renovate it. Soon there would be a new pier with neon lights and restaurants with waiters. No more cotton candy. No more corn dogs. It was cold in the shadows, and she began to run.

The bell jangled above Phil's door as she pushed it open, and there was the warm, musty, dusty smell that belonged only to Phil's. Yellowed photographs smiled from the faded walls.

"Phil?" Coline called.

"I'm in the back."

The old man knelt before a half-filled carton. A stripe of sunlight silvered what was left of his hair and turned his glasses into mirrors.

"You know?" Coline asked.

Phil sat back on his heels. "I was at the meeting till three this morning. We've got ten days."

"It's not fair." Coline kicked at one of the boxes.

Phil spread his hands, palms up, and smiled.

Coline picked up one of the pictures that lay on the floor, ready for packing. She struggled with her voice. "Who's this, Phil? Tallulah?"

Phil put out a hand for the picture. "No. No. That's Constance." His voice remembered. "She came to the pier, way back. I guess it was in the thirties. She had her two little girls with her, and they each had a fur hat and a muff, white as snow. They rode the Merry-Go-Round, all three of them, and she was laughing and screaming as loud as the children." He wiped dust from the glass with the sleeve of his sweater. "Then they came and had me take their picture. All the stars liked to do that." He layered the photograph in newspaper and put it in the box. "That's the way it was, once upon a time."

Coline walked to the small window. A barge headed out to sea, followed by a skyful of screeching, squabbling gulls. "What will you do, Phil?"

"Get me a place close by where I can hang my pictures. Come down here, sit on the new pier."

"I'll come visit you, Phil. You'll be lonely." She swung around at Phil's bark of laughter.

"Come and be welcome, Coline. But don't expect me to be lonely." His hands swept to the filled cartons, the faded patches on the walls where the pictures had hung, the window that let in the outside life of the pier. "I'm taking it all with me."

"But, Phil!" There were things Coline wanted to say. They're dead, these people. Gone. The pier was your life for sixty years.

It'll be gone, too. "It's not right," she said. "They're taking it all from you."

"Nobody can take anything I don't want to give." Phil tapped a finger against the side of his head. "It's in here. That's what people mean when they talk about living forever." He touched his head again. "All my life is up here."

Coline turned back to the window. Two boys, barefoot, swung the big telescope around, checking the beach and the ocean and the hill beyond. Saturday, and the people were coming.

"Yes," Coline thought. "Yes."

She lifted one finger and secretly touched her forehead. It was in there. The windows filled with dried starfish and coconut monkeys. The pickles and the spiced mustard. And the Merry-Go-Round.

She closed her eyes and the horses went up and down, round and around. Leo and Sissy and pretty white Dulcie. The stirrups too long for the feet to reach. The music, going faster and faster. She'd never forget it. The pier had happened and she had happened and they were a part of each other. No one could take it away.

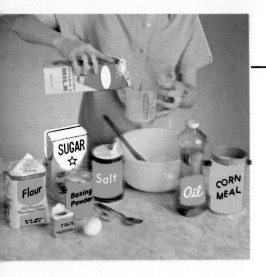

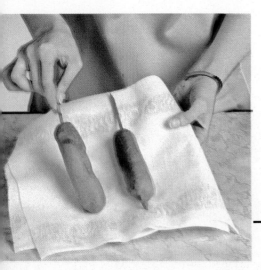

Corn Dogs

a pound of hot dogs

wooden skewers

oil for frying

corn-meal batter

How to make corn-meal batter:

Stir well together ½ cup of flour, ⅓ cup of corn meal, 1 tablespoon of sugar, 2 teaspoons of dry mustard, 1 teaspoon of baking powder, ½ teaspoon of salt, 1 tablespoon of oil, ½ cup of milk, and 1 egg. Makes one cup of batter.

Directions for corn dogs:

Dry hot dogs on paper towels and insert a skewer in one end of each hot dog. Dip each hot dog in batter, coating completely. (Pour batter in a tall drinking glass for easy coating.) Fry in deep hot fat (375°) until golden, about two minutes. Drain on paper towels.

Farthest West Village

by Lael Morgan

Atka is a tiny village far out on Alaska's Aleutian Islands chain. Not counting the U.S. Navy base at Adak, it is the westernmost settlement in the United States. It has no airstrip and no real dock. There is no post office, no telephones, and no electricity. The only link with the outside world is through a cranky 50-watt radio. The only way to get to Atka is by Navy tug, which makes the 100-mile round trip from Adak every month or so, weather permitting. And the weather in the Aleutians is about the worst in the world.

"Qas! Qas!" Danny Boy Snigaroff yells excitedly in his native Aleut (AL-ee-oot) language to his friend Michael Dirks. "Fish! Fish!"

Four Alaskan "humpy" salmon, the first of the season, are splashing up the swift river. They are early, and the boys don't have fishing poles with them.

Quickly, they take their hunting knives and tie them to long poles with their boot laces. Then, jumping into the icy water, they throw their spears just as Aleut hunters did more than two hundred years ago.

"I've got one!" Danny Boy yells to Michael, who has waded further upstream.

"Me too!" shouts Michael, triumphantly waving a wiggling two-foot-long fish on his makeshift spear.

Danny Boy and Michael live in the village of Atka in Alaska's Aleutian Islands. Thousands of years ago, their Eskimo ancestors settled the whole big chain of islands, traveling hundreds of miles over stormy seas in their light walrus-skin boats called *kayaks*. The Aleut hunters were skillful, and their warriors strong and bold.

The little village of Atka is one of the last Aleut strongholds. Its eighty-seven residents, of Aleut-Russian stock, draw their living mainly from the land and sea—hunting and fishing. But because Atka is very poor and has no paying jobs, many of its workers must seek jobs far from home, for at least part of the year, to support their families. This means that the children left behind must work hard, hunting and fishing and helping out at home.

But Danny Boy and Michael are proud of their lifestyle and their responsibilities. Sometimes their older brothers take them hunting for wild reindeer in the island's mountain ranges or for walrus and seal along the

rocky coast. Both boys already can handle a gun and row a small boat in rough seas. Before long, they hope they'll shoot their first big game.

All this is work. For although it sounds like sport to us, it's serious business for young Aleuts who must help support their families. But growing up on a big wild island can be a lot of fun, too. Near the village is a three-mile stretch of beach for treasure hunting. There, the Bering Sea often tosses up Japanese fishing floats of colored glass, nets, weird old pieces of machinery, and wrecks of ships. And nearby there's a ghost town—an old military base that the United States abandoned after World War II—that's great for exploring.

In the winter the children slide on steep snow-covered hills, and in the summer they slide downhill, too—using cardboard over slippery green grasses.

The children also like to go hiking. There are lakes for swimming, bubbling springs of hot water, giant water-falls, and many mountains to climb. There's even a white-coned volcano that rumbles so loud it scares the reindeer—but it never blows up.

Best of all, Danny Boy and Michael like "cliff-hanging." The previous summer a visiting geologist showed them how real mountain climbers wrap ropes around their bodies to pull themselves up and down steep rock walls. The boys have gotten so good at moun-tain climbing that they can make their way right to the top of a peak with no foothold at all—right up beside the nest of a high-flying eagle! They call their favorite climb-ing spot Tarzan's Place.

Like youngsters everywhere, Danny Boy and Michael have to go to school. But even school is different in Atka. Where else do kids get to make up their own school-books?

In 1973 the Alaska legislature passed a law that al-lows native languages to be taught in Alaska's schools right along with English. While the people of Atka were very pleased with this new law, it presented a problem because their Aleut language had never been written down. There wasn't even an alphabet, so one had to be invented.

That summer Michael's older brother, Moses, and Danny Boy's big sister, Sally, got together with the village secretary, Mrs. Nadesta Golley, to work out the words in the new alphabet. Then the students at Atka's grade school helped in making up stories and in creating illustrations for schoolbooks. And the whole package was bundled up and sent off to be printed in Fairbanks by the Eskimo, Indian, Aleut Printing Co., which is producing bilingual books for schools all over Alaska.

The inventors of the Atka alphabet found they even had to make up some new letters to handle the soft sounds of their dialect of the Aleut language. For example, an *x* with a "hat" on it ($\hat{x}$) represents a sort of breathy sound. Aleut is a quiet language—one that is almost impossible to shout—and the words often sound like the things they name. Listen as you say these words in Aleut:

wind—slagux (sluh-HOH)	fish—qas (KWAH)
water—taangax (TUHNG-ah)	yes—aang (UHNG)
school—achixaalux (ah-CHIG-uh-luk)	

Don't ask what the word is for "no." There isn't any word for "no" in the dialect spoken on Atka. (Although now that the people are writing stories and books, they're thinking about borrowing a "no" from a neighboring dialect.)

Even with the harsh life on that lonely island, there's no word for "suffering." Nor is there a word for "goodbye"—although the people will tell you that having to leave the island is the hardest part about life in Atka. And leaving is something Danny Boy and Michael will have to face soon. To go to high school, they will have to live at either Adak or Anchorage, a thousand miles away.

For now, however, the boys will wait and see before deciding what to do. They've read about the rest of the world, and they'd like to have a look at some of it. But they're still pretty sure Atka must be one of the very best places to live—especially when the first salmon come swimming up the river and your aim is good.

The Wonderful World of Words

Words! Words! Words! What are they? Where do they come from? The people of Atka discovered some interesting facts when they tried to make a written language.

The world of words is fascinating because words are only symbols that are used to express ideas. No matter what their culture is or where they live, people have a need to express many similar thoughts. Look at the chart below, and you will see how people of different lands say the same thing.

Make a large copy of the chart for the classroom. If there are classmates who can speak other languages, invite them to add the words they use to express the ideas on the chart. Learn to use these words in class and with your friends.

English	Spanish	French	Polish
Hello	Hola (OH-lah)	Bonjour (bohn-ZHOOR)	Dziendobry (jayn-DOH-bree)
Good-bye	Adios (AH-dee-OHS)	Au revoir (oh-ruh-VWAHR)	Dowidzenia (doh-vee-DZEN-yah)
Please	Por favor (por-fa-VOR)	S'il vous plaît (seel-voo-PLE)	Prosze (PROH-she)
Thank you	Gracias (GRAH-see-ahs)	Merci (mer-SEE)	Dziekuje (jen-KOO-ye)

Another fact that the people of Atka discovered is that words are often borrowed from other languages. Many of our words have traveled far and can tell exciting stories about their origin.

For example, the word *volcano* is named after Vulcan, the Roman god of fire. He was the son of Jupiter, lord of the gods. Vulcan's workroom was inside the top of a very high mountain, where he made armor for all the gods. To make the armor, he kept a very hot fire burning inside the mountain.

One day Vulcan took sides in a battle against Jupiter. Jupiter became so angry that he threw Vulcan off the top of the mountain.

That was how a mountain that throws out fire and lava came to be called a volcano. The word was borrowed from the Latin word *Vulcanus* (Vulcan).

Look in the library, in books of word origins, or in large dictionaries to find more stories of word origins. Make a chart to show the information you find. For example,

Word	Origin	Meaning	How the word got its present meaning
pencil	Latin word *penicillus*	"little tail"	The word was first applied to a brush of fine hair used by artists. *Pen* comes from a Latin word meaning "feather." The first pens were feathers.

Illustrate your chart and share it with your friends.

The Bird Artist of the High Arctic

George Miksch Sutton was a writer, a teacher, and a bird artist known the world over. He made more than fifteen expeditions over the Far North. He always carried with him his paint box, huge sheets of paper for on-the-scene sketches, and a notebook for his day-to-day observations. He made hundreds of bird drawings. Many have been displayed in museums and art galleries.

When asked how he became interested in his work, Dr. Sutton replied, "I have been drawing birds since I was five years old. My first serious drawing was of a prize rooster at a Nebraska state fair. An admiring passer-by paid a dime for it."

In his book *High Arctic*, Dr. Sutton tells about his experiences and adventures across the islands of the Canadian North. The story "Adventure in the High Arctic" tells about one of Dr. Sutton's experiences on Bathurst Island.

Adventure in the High Arctic

by George Miksch Sutton

The station of Eureka was not far from the shore of the fiords near the mouth of a shallow brook. Beyond the brook was rolling country in which Dave and Phil planned to record the flight songs of knots. Attracted to the gentle slope between the landing strip and Blacktop Ridge, I decided to go that way by myself. I took binoculars, but no gun. I had been sitting still for hours, so I needed a walk.

On the road to the landing strip, I was overwhelmed by three big huskies who were just as eager to stretch their legs as I was. They gathered around my feet, hindering every step. As I yelled, "Stay home!" and waved my arms, the huskies bounced off gleefully, only to bounce back again. I started to pick up a rock, and the largest husky tried to get the rock for me. He gave my neck a noisy lick while I was leaning over and punched me so hard with his nose that I almost fell down. When I straightened up, he gave my right hand an oddly loving nuzzle that seemed to say "Think nothing of it. You know I mean well."

235

I could not understand why the dogs were so eager to go along. They had all the time any dog could want, now that it was summer. The whole outdoors was theirs. It must have been the companionship that they craved. They needed the joy of sharing with another mortal the bright sky, the wind, and the spicy fragrance of the tiny white arctic heather bells.

By the time I reached the landing strip, the huskies were no longer bothersome. They had scattered a bit—the serious-minded husky had gone ahead; one husky had stayed behind, limping a little; and the biggest husky was a few feet away from me, eager to come closer if I gave it the slightest encouragement.

Somewhat to my relief, the huskies started to walk away. I was tempted to call them back, especially the big one that I'd grown to like, but I let them go. Smaller and smaller they became. They looked like toy huskies as they climbed a shoulder of the slope far to my right and disappeared. How uneventful life promised to be without them.

I had no desire to climb Blacktop, but I did want to reach ground that was high enough and would permit me to look down on the station, fiord, and landing strip all at one time. Knowing that sooner or later I would have to cross the gully, I walked up to the foot of the ridge.

Walking was tricky, for the spongy hummocks were so far apart that each step required a look, a push with one foot, and a sort of reaching out and grabbing with the other. The stream bed was dry.

On higher land at last, I looked down over the slopes below me. For a time I failed to notice a band of musk oxen, all at rest. They were on flat ground at a slightly higher level, several hundred yards away. Most of the nine animals appeared to be fully adult. But one musk ox was somewhat undersized, a yearling perhaps, and another one was a very young calf.

While I was looking the musk oxen over, one by one, through binoculars, a gray-white dog ran toward the musk oxen. He was plainly not one of the three huskies that had accompanied me. Quickly the musk oxen arose and formed a circle. Now I could not see the calf at all. The head of every animal was lowered, ready for action.

My reaction was unpleasant. Suddenly I felt responsible and guilty. This dog may have followed the other three huskies. They probably had come along with me against station rules. That was the reason for their being so gleeful! Now there'd be trouble. Either a musk ox would be

hurt or at least one dog would be hurt or killed. And I'd
be to blame. I should have made it clear that I was going
for a walk and that it was not my wish nor my inten-
tion to take the dogs along.

I was much too far away to try calling the gray-white
dog back. Furthermore, I knew that the gray-white dog
would pay no more attention to me than the other three
dogs had. "Oh, well," I told myself as I headed back for
the station. I was hoping against hope that all the dogs
would follow. Those huskies must surely have chased
musk oxen around here before, and the musk oxen must
surely have learned how to deal with them.

There was a good reason for this thinking, for the gray-white dog, tired of running around the horned circle, was now trotting off. And the circle had broken up. I could see the calf once more. It was a tiny thing, slightly darker than the older animals.

An hour later, back at the station, I asked, "How many dogs do you have here?"

Someone answered, "Three. They all went with you. They love to get out, you know."

The gray-white "dog" had been a wolf. It was something I should have known, for its tail had not curled, huskie fashion, up over its back.

Soap Sculpture

Imagine yourself in the High Arctic with George Miksch Sutton. Make a soap sculpture of something you saw. Here are directions for making a soap Eskimo. A soap dog, bird, or musk ox can be made the same way.

Get a bar of soap, a knife, a pin, and one piece of paper.

Do this:

- Rule half-inch squares on paper that is the size of the bar of soap.
- Draw the figure on the paper, using the squares as guides.
- Place the paper on the soap, and use the pin to dot the outline of the figure through the paper into the soap.
- Remove the paper from the soap.
- Use the knife to follow the outline of the dots to cut away the soap and round the figure on all sides.
- Polish the figure by rubbing it with your finger.
- Exhibit your soap sculpture.

The TIME of KAAMOS

by M. A. Crane

"Ted! Are you daydreaming?" Kris Sakki paused in his fence mending to glance over at Ted.

Ted Young shook his head. He was too cold and sorry for himself to be daydreaming. Along the reindeer fence, Mr. Sakki was explaining something to Ted's father, while Mr. Young snapped photographs of the antlered beasts. Erik Sakki knew all about reindeer—as all Lapps did.

Ted stamped in the snow as hard as his skis would allow. This trip to Finland with his father, a photographer for a large American magazine, had been a great adventure at first. That is, until Mr. Young had met Kris's father at the Lapp Reindeer Roundup.

"These roundup photographs are taken by tourists," Mr. Sakki had said. "Why don't you come to my place? You can live with us, the true Lapp way. We are far away from civilization, and you can see the land on which the reindeer run. It will give you a good story for your magazine, I think."

Mr. Young had thought so, too, and he had accepted the invitation. At first, Ted thought it was fun, but after a week in the smoky Lapp house, he was ready to go home.

The Sakkis had few modern conveniences. They ate mostly reindeer stew, which seemed fatty to Ted; and none of them except Kris and his father spoke any English. It was unsettling—not being able to understand when they spoke Lapp around him—and the visit included a lot of work, too.

Ted was expected to spend some time chopping wood. More important, he was supposed to help family members inspect and repair the fences that penned the reindeer. It was hard just following the Sakkis around on skis in the cold, dark world that was Lapland. There was no such thing as amusement. No television, no——

"No fun at all," Ted grumbled, as his father and Erik Sakki glided toward him on their skis.

"That's all for today," Mr. Young was saying. "I got some excellent shots. Erik, this certainly was a splendid idea."

"Ah," Mr. Sakki smiled, "now we'll go homeward. It is very dark out here."

"How do you like these long winters, Kris?" asked Mr. Young.

Kris smiled. "We call it the *Kaamos*—the dark period. I suppose strangers may think it grim, but in frosty weather we have the northern lights. It's really beautiful out here. And in summer, arctic heather makes the ground grow red."

Inside the house, Kris's mother brought them cups of hot coffee, with sugar cubes to hold between their teeth as they drank the hot liquid. She asked a question, and Erik replied. He motioned Ted and his father to be seated by the fire.

Suddenly, Ted could not help himself. "Why do you live way out here, anyway?" he asked. "I mean far away from everything that's any fun. You work all winter and summer chasing reindeer, and——"

"Ted!" Mr. Young said sternly, but the Sakkis didn't mind.

"To a Lapp, this is the only way to live," Erik said. "Reindeer are our way of life, Ted—our money, our food and clothing. What do you call 'fun' in your country?"

"Well," Ted shrugged helplessly, "you've been in Finland, and seen big cities. There are movies, and—and—" he floundered under Kris's amused smile.

"If you stay here long enough, I'll show you something better than any movie," the Lapp boy promised. "Ah, here are my uncles."

Erik Sakki's brothers Mikael and Johann entered, looking like huge, colorful bears in their work clothes. They spoke hurriedly in Lapp.

"Is anything wrong?" Mr. Young inquired.

"Yes," Erik Sakki nodded. "Some reindeer escaped through a break in the north side of the fence. Mikael and Johann got most of them back in and repaired the fence. But three are still out. They can't have gotten far. Kris, think you can handle it?"

"All alone?" Ted gasped.

"Of course. Unless you'd like to go with him."

Though Mr. Sakki smiled, Ted sensed that this was a kind of challenge to him.

"Sure," he said. "I'll go with Kris."

Outside in the unchanging darkness, the boys strapped on their skis. Then Ted asked, "Why must you rescue the reindeer when your father and uncles are inside?"

"Father and my uncles have been working all day, and they are tired. I spent most of the day with you instead of working. But don't worry," Kris reassured him, "I've done this many times."

He skied off. Ted was a good skier, but he could never match the grace that Kris had. He followed the Lapp boy over the snow, between groups of small evergreen trees.

For a half hour they cruised along. Suddenly, Kris stopped.

"There they are! I think they're all does."

For a moment Ted could see nothing. Then he made out three dark shapes against the snow in a hollow between two gentle slopes.

"Do we round them up, or what?" Ted asked.

Before Kris could answer, the animals began to snort nervously.

"What's wrong with them?" Ted asked. He wondered if reindeer had ever charged their herders.

"Something frightened them just now, and I'm afraid it's wolves! I didn't bring my rifle!" Kris's voice was sharp with dismay. "We'll have to drive them off." Two smaller dark shapes were loping over the snow.

Kris pointed. "Ted, go that way, and make noise. Sound as loud and fierce as you can. I'll go the other way. Maybe we can scare them."

"Won't the deer run?"

"They might. Anyway, we've got to save them one way or another!" Kris bent his slight form and was gone. Ted hesitated for a moment, took a deep breath, and pushed off. He stared at the loping wolves and back toward the panicky animals. Suddenly, he felt exactly as Kris did. The reindeer had to be protected!

Waving his ski pole, Ted yelled, "Get out! Scat! Yah-h-h!"

On the other slope Kris was making a similar commotion. The reindeer snorted and pawed but huddled closer together. The wolves halted and then came on, a bit more warily.

Ted pushed himself forward once more. Now he was almost near enough to strike one of the wolves with his pole. He gave another wild yell that echoed across the snow.

The wolves backed off a little. Then they turned tail and slowly trotted away.

Now that it was over, Ted's legs began to tremble. Both boys turned on their skis and headed down toward the reindeer.

"Why d-didn't the wolves attack us?" Ted asked at last.

"They couldn't have been really hungry. Otherwise, we'd have had no chance against them." Kris's voice was angry. "I was foolish not to have brought the rifle!"

245

Ted was about to speak when, suddenly, Kris pointed skyward. Slight ripples of green light were playing across the darkness.

As the boys watched, the bands of light unfolded into green and yellow waves that rose higher and higher into the sky until the darkness seemed to be lighted by a hundred flickering candles.

"The northern lights!" Kris said, his voice full of pride.

Ted nodded. He understood at last why Kris loved this harsh, cold land. He could understand why Kris's Lapp ancestors had continued to follow their herds across the country, protecting them from attacking wolves. He felt proud that for a short time he had been a part of the Lapps and had protected the reindeer herd.

"It's time to get started," he said. Without thinking he added, "Our deer are getting tired just standing there—"

He broke off, embarrassed, but Kris didn't seem to have noticed. "You are right," he agreed, "and the family will be waiting for us to come home!"

A Game of the Far North

Bilboquet, also known as ring and pin, is a game that is played in many parts of the world. During the dark months of the long arctic winter, the people of the Far North enjoy this pastime.

The Eskimos call the game *ajaquq*. The ring and pin are carved from the bones of the animals they hunt. The object of the game is to catch the ring on the pin, which is held in your hand. The trick looks simple enough when an Eskimo does it, but it is not easily learned. Those who master the art have every right to be proud of their skill.

Are you as skilled as the people of the arctic lands? Find out by making your own ring-and-pin game and playing it.

Get the things you need.
    plastic straw   paper cup
    two pieces of string about twelve inches long
    tag-board paper   scissors   pencil

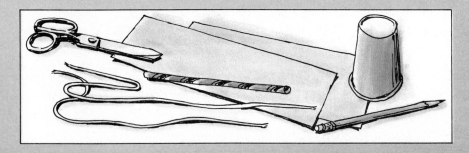

Do this:

- Place the cup upside down on the tag board.
- Make a "ring" by tracing around the rim of the cup, then cutting out the circle. Trace and cut out one more ring the same way.
- Cut out the inside of each ring, leaving a half-inch rim.
- Tie one end of the string to the ring and the other end to the "pin" (straw). Do the same with the other ring and the other piece of string.

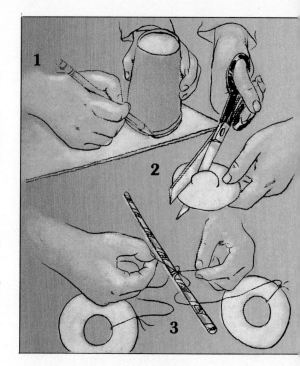

Play the game:

- Hold one ring against the pin.
- Try to get the other ring on the pin by swinging it above the pin.
- Once the ring is caught on the pin, try to catch the second ring while the first one is on the pin.
- The game is over when both rings are caught.
- For an extra challenge, have a friend use a timer to tell you how long it takes you to get both rings on the pin. Try to beat your own record the next time.

Good luck!

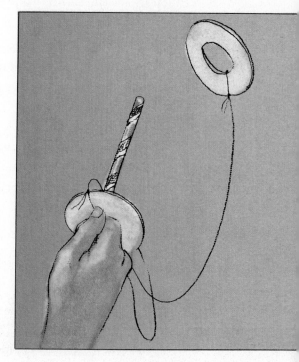

In Search of a Pharaoh

On October 28, 1922, archaeologist Howard Carter called the foreman of his excavating crew and told him to begin work without delay. Carter knew that he had less than two months to complete the search that he had been involved in for ten years—the search for the tomb of Tutankhamen, who had ruled in Egypt more than three thousand years before.

Carter had just returned from a meeting in England with the earl of Carnarvon, who had been paying the excavation cost. Carnarvon, disappointed by years of failure, told Carter that he had decided not to reapply for the government grant to excavate in the Valley of the Kings. But Carter pleaded. He offered to pay the cost himself if nothing was found. Finally, Carnarvon agreed to one final season of excavating, or digging, in the valley.

More than three thousand years ago, the Valley of the Kings in Egypt was the royal necropolis, or the burial place of kings. Archaeologists, who study how people lived in the past, had long been interested in excavating in this area. It had been part of ancient Thebes, the capital from which the Egyptian empire was ruled at the height of its political power.

Archaeologists had already found about thirty-three royal tombs in the valley. But most of those had been robbed by thieves many years before. Experts believed that all the treasures of the burial ground had been found.

Howard Carter, who had spent more than thirty years in Egypt, disagreed. He was certain that there were parts of the valley that were not explored. After studying a list of kings, or pharaohs, of Egypt, Carter was convinced that Tutankhamen's tomb was hidden somewhere in the valley.

According to studies, Tutankhamen became king at the age of eight or nine, in about 1334 B.C. His parentage is uncertain, but it is known that he was married while still a child to Ankhesenamen, the third daughter of the famous Nefertiti.

The reign of Tutankhamen lasted only about nine years. He died when he was seventeen or eighteen. The cause of his death is unknown.

Even if Tutankhamen's tomb lay in the valley, Carter faced a difficult task looking for it. Tons of rock and sand would have to be removed by workers filling baskets, carrying them to vacant ground, emptying them, and returning—actions that would be slowly and laboriously repeated millions of times.

Now Carter was facing his last chance to find the tomb. After the conversation with his foreman, work was begun. Fifty workers began digging in search of the tomb.

Within the next few days of the dig, a layer of flint chips was uncovered. It was an encouraging discovery, since this type of rock was often used to block the entrance of royal tombs.

Finally, a trench had been dug. One morning when Carter arrived, he found his workers just standing around.

"By the solemn silence all around caused by the stoppage of work, I guessed that something out of the usual had occurred," Carter wrote later. "My [foreman] was most cheerful, and confidentially told me that the beginning of a staircase had been discovered . . ."

Working slowly and carefully, the workers began clearing the staircase, which led deep into the ground. At the level of the twelfth stair, the top of a doorway came into view. On the blocked and sealed door were the seals of the royal necropolis—the jackal-god Anubis above nine defeated enemies.

"It was a thrilling moment for an excavator in that valley of unutterable silence," Carter wrote, "suddenly to find himself, after so many years of toilsome work, on the verge of what looked like a magnificent discovery."

Even during that moment of discovery, Carter had doubts that this was the tomb of Tutankhamen. The entrance seemed too modest to be the tomb of a king. Carter thought it might have been a hiding place of royal objects or the tomb of a royal relative. But what seemed important was that no one had known it was there.

Carter could have continued to dig to satisfy his curiosity, but he ordered the stairway filled again. He posted guards and hurried to send a message to Carnarvon. It read, "At last have made wonderful discovery in valley; a magnificent tomb with seals intact; re-covered same for your arrival; congratulations."

Carnarvon replied that he would arrive in Alexandria with his daughter, Lady Evelyn Herbert. Since this was long before the days of air travel, it took several weeks for Carnarvon and his daughter to arrive from England. Almost immediately after their arrival, they traveled to the site of the excavation. Carter and the workers had begun clearing the stairway again. As more of the doorway was uncovered, the seals of Tutankhamen could be seen, as well as those of the royal necropolis. When all sixteen steps had been cleared of rock and the entire doorway could be seen, Carter was taken aback. Holes had been cut into part of the door. The damage had been repaired and bore the seals of the necropolis, but the questions remained: Had this tomb, too, been robbed? Had he worked this hard to find nothing?

The work continued, and the door was removed, revealing a passageway filled with rubble. But there were indications that a tunnel had been cut through the filling, thousands of years before. The passage was cleared. At its end was another sealed doorway twenty-five feet from the entrance, but it too had been cut through and repaired.

"The next day following," Carter wrote of November 26, "was the day of days, the most wonderful that I had ever lived through."

With Carnarvon and his daughter standing nearby, Carter made a small hole in the top of the door.

"Darkness and blank space, as far as an iron testing-rod could reach, showed that whatever lay beyond was empty," he wrote. "Widening the hole a little, I inserted the candle and peered in . . . At first I could see nothing, the hot air escaping from the chamber causing the candle flame to flicker, but presently, as my eyes grew accustomed to the light, details of the room within emerged slowly from the mist, strange animals, statues, and gold—everywhere the glint of gold."

Lord Carnarvon, unable to contain his excitement any longer, asked, "Can you see anything?" Carter answered slowly, "Yes, wonderful things."

When Carter's eyes grew accustomed to the dim light, he gazed upon priceless objects in the Antechamber, which looked like the back room of a rummage shop. The objects that would comprise the greatest find in the history

of archaeology were piled one upon another in untidy heaps. Among the objects were parts of three ceremonial beds, gold thrones, shrines, vases, chariots, magnificently inlaid boxes, statuettes, weapons, and many other objects of wealth, power, and religious significance. Carter concluded that the tomb had been robbed, most likely within a short time after the burial. The thieves had carried away gold stones and objects that were small, valuable, and easy to carry. Many gold-covered treasures had to be left behind because they were too heavy to carry.

Carter and his workers went no further that day. Demanding work would be needed in order for this find to be handled with the care it deserved. Even so, Carter hardly imagined that this work would occupy him for the next ten years.

Carter's workers put up two heavy wooden doors that blocked the tomb. They were locked, and only Carter's most trustworthy assistants remained on guard. Every possible measure was taken to preserve the priceless objects that had lain there since the days that the pharaohs ruled Egypt.

Reports of the discovery spread very quickly, and newspapers from all over the world announced it in their headlines. Tourists and curiosity seekers thronged to the valley to catch a glimpse of the rich and mysterious treasures. Carnarvon decided that the time had come for an official announcement. It was made at the tomb on November 29, 1922.

Carter knew he would need technical assistance for the excavation. He did not hesitate to seek it. Since this was a discovery perhaps never to be repeated in history, each object had to be labeled, recorded, and photographed. Descriptive notes had to be made of everything.

Carter bought many bales of cotton and miles of bandages, packing boxes, and lumber for wrapping and packing the treasures before they could be transported to a museum.

The removal of the contents of the Antechamber required several weeks of careful work. When the Antechamber was cleared, Carter focused his attention on the two sealed chambers that led off it. Both had also been entered by thieves. Carter looked first into the room across from the entrance, which he termed the Annex. It was found to contain articles similar to those in the Antechamber. It was in the other chamber, which opened

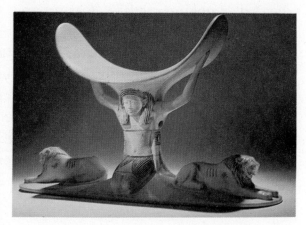

off the right wall, that Carter decided they would find Tutankhamen's tomb. That was where they went to work next.

On February 17, 1923, the Burial Chamber was ready to be opened. Carter was there, along with twenty experts and Egyptian government officials who filled the Antechamber. Hundreds of people stood outside.

Carter carefully chipped away at the stone and plaster with which the doorway to the Burial Chamber had been covered. "The temptation to stop and peer inside at every moment was irresistible," he wrote. "And, when, after about ten minutes' work, I had made a hole large enough to enable me to do so, I inserted an electric torch. An astonishing sight its light revealed, for there, within a yard of the entrance of the chamber, stood what to appearance was a solid wall of gold."

The dazzled Carter quickly chipped away the rest of the filling. When he stepped inside, he realized that what he was looking at was one side of a huge gilt shrine that covered the sarcophagus of Tutankhamen. Made of wood covered with gold, it measured seventeen by eleven feet and was nine feet high. It filled the room except for a space about two feet wide between its sides and the rock walls. In one wall was another doorway. It was unsealed. Looking within, Carter and Carnarvon saw still another astounding sight.

"Facing the doorway, on the farther side, stood the most beautiful monument that I have ever seen," he wrote. "The central portion of it consisted of a large shrine-shaped chest, completely overlaid with gold . . . Surrounding this, free-standing, were statues of four goddesses of the dead—gracious figures with outstretched protective arms, so natural and lifelike in their pose . . ."

It was not until the following season that the shrine and three others inside it were entered. Then the huge stone lid of the sarcophagus was lifted to reveal the pharaoh's coffin. Two other coffins were nested inside it. The innermost one was made of solid gold, beautifully engraved, about one eighth of an inch thick. Within lay the linen-covered body of Tutankhamen, looked upon by mortal eyes for the first time in more than three thousand years. Covering his head and shoulders was one of the greatest artistic treasures—the polished gold mask, elegant, calm, yet breathing with the life of a supremacy that had ended thousands of years before.

Carter's discovery led to a great amount of knowledge about a cultural existence that would have otherwise been unknown. Even the smallest objects revealed something to the modern world about a civilization that existed more than three thousand years ago. The one-time pharaoh and the priceless collection of treasures now rest at a museum in Cairo.

A Discovered Past

While excavating in Egypt's Valley of the Kings, archaeologist Howard Carter and his workers made the discovery of the century—the ancient tomb of Tutankhamen. The men encountered a world that existed thousands of years ago. Their world came together with the past when they discovered many wonderful and unusual things.

Below are some of the things that Carter and his workers found when they were working in the valley. See how many of these things you can identify. Read each sentence. Then look at the pictures to find the one that best fits each description. Rewrite each sentence on a piece of paper. Look in an encyclopedia or in a book about Egypt to check your answers.

An object that shows human workmanship is called an ___.

A ___ was an ancient king of Egypt.

Pictures, characters, or symbols used in Egyptian writing are called ___.

pharaoh   hieroglyphics   artifact

If you want to have fun with your friends, make a "Did You Know" book about Tutankhamen, or King Tut. Do these things:

- Look in the encyclopedia or in books about Egypt to find some interesting and descriptive facts about King Tutankhamen or events that happened during his rule.
- Organize the information you gathered.
- Write each fact or piece of information on a separate piece of paper. On the back of the paper, draw a picture to accompany your fact.

front	back
Did you know that King Tut had to learn to read when he was four years old? *He spent many years making thousands of hieroglyphics.*	 Hieroglyphics representing King Tutankhamen's name

- Place all the papers together, being careful to keep all the edges straight.
- Design a cover.
- Staple your book together.

When you have completed your book, place it on the reading table or the library table for everyone to enjoy.

A Reading Entertainment Bureau

Organize a student entertainment bureau to provide ideas for class presentations or for parent meetings. Find stories, games, and reading activities that you think are fun and that you think other students will enjoy.

Talk with your teacher about the idea, then interest some friends in helping you.

You and your friends might start by looking through the Contents pages for stories and activities you have enjoyed. Each of you should choose something that you liked best. Then think how you might share it with other classes. Use your knowledge and imagination. Write your ideas on cards and keep a file.

Suppose that you have chosen the story "Sasquatch: Creature of the North." You might tape the story. Then read "Agent Whiteclaw's Special Report." Have the code available so that you can show how to do the secret writing. Before taping the story, practice reading it aloud until you are sure you can make it sound exciting.

If someone chooses the story "Slideout," he or she could prepare an exhibit of different kinds of motorcycles. Toy models, pictures, or drawings could be used.

If you were to tell the story of Louise Scherbyn, you could demonstrate the "Describe-a-Person" puzzle. Then ask the audience to think of another sports hero or heroine. Help them work out a description of that person the same way as the puzzle.

After telling the story "The Toys," you could demonstrate how to cut a party mask. Then let your audience try making masks of their liking.

Parents would enjoy sharing with you the story "Remembrance of Things Past." Tell the story and invite parents to play one of the games. Then give them the opportunity to tell about and demonstrate some of their favorite games when they were your age.

You could use different methods for presenting these stories—tapes, puppets, choral readings, dramatizations, radio or television shows, or other ideas that come to you.

When everyone is ready, present the selections to your audience. This can be a group of students in another class, parents, or friends.

Keep adding cards to your file as you and your friends prepare more selections.

Books for You

Come Back, Peter by Joan Woodberry

A rebellious Paul sets out on a camping trip, where he meets two courageous children who have journeyed through a hot, waterless plain in order to find help for a sick mother.

The Slave Dancer by Paula Fox

This award-winning story is about thirteen-year-old Jessie Bollier, who is kidnaped and carried across the ocean to the coast of Africa.

Graciela by Joe Molnar

How is your background similar to or different from that of a twelve-year-old Mexican-American girl? In this story, Graciela talks about her family life, her hobbies, and her aspirations for the future.

Journey to America by Sonia Levitin

Lisa Platt, a young Jewish girl, and her family from Germany must leave everything behind to begin again in new surroundings.

The Dastardly Murder of Dirty Pete by Eth Clifford

Two sisters and their father set off on a vacation to the West Coast. They encounter many adventures when they get lost in a ghost town.

(Acknowledgments continued from page 2.)

Doubleday & Company, Inc. for "Slideout" from MOTORCYCLE RACER by John P. Covington. Copyright © 1973 by Doubleday & Company, Inc. Reprinted by permission of Doubleday & Company, Inc.

Paul S. Eriksson, Publisher for "The Bird Artist of the High Arctic" and "Adventure in the High Arctic." Adapted from HIGH ARCTIC: AN EXPEDITION TO THE UNSPOILED NORTH by George Miksch Sutton. Copyright © 1971. Used by permission of Paul S. Eriksson, Publisher.

Harcourt Brace Jovanovich, Inc. and Hogarth Press for "The Toys." From THE TREASURE OF LI-PO by Alice Ritchie, copyright, 1949, by Harcourt Brace Jovanovich, Inc.; renewed, 1977, by M.T. Ritchie. Reprinted by permission of the publishers.

Instructor for "California Gold." Adapted from HISTORY ON STAGE by Barbara Friedmann and Jennifer Phelps. Reprinted from INSTRUCTOR CURRICULUM MATERIALS, 1975. Copyright © 1975 by The Instructor Publication, Inc. Used by permission.

Lerner Publications Company for "Motorcycle Races" by Nicole Puleo from MOTORCYCLE RACING by Nicole Puleo. Copyright © 1973 by Lerner Publications Company, 241 First Avenue North, Minneapolis, Minnesota 55401.

Lucinda Oakland Morken for permission to adapt "The Gold Maker." From Young World magazine, copyright © 1973 by The Saturday Evening Post Company.

QED Publishing Limited for "The Story of Money." Adapted from THE BOOK OF MONEY edited by Klaus Heidensohn. Copyright © 1979. Used by permission of QED Publishing Limited.

Random House, Inc. for "The Batboy Who Played." Adapted by permission of Random House, Inc. from STRANGE BUT TRUE BASEBALL STORIES, by Furman Bisher. Copyright © 1966 by Random House, Inc.

Road Rider magazine for "The Touring Biker's Highway" by Don Smith and "Louise Scherbyn: Pioneer Cyclist" by Alice Turner. Copyright © 1974 by Roger Hull. Reprinted from Road Rider magazine, Post Office Box 678, South Laguna, California 92677.

St. Martin's Press, Inc. for "Street Games" from WHAT DID YOU DO WHEN YOU WERE A KID? by Fred Sturner, copyright © 1973. Used by permission of St. Martin's Press, Inc.

The Saturday Evening Post Company for "The Time of Kaamos" from Jack and Jill magazine. Copyright © 1970 by The Holiday Publishing Company, Inc.; for "A Pot of Water for Bokkas," from Child Life magazine. Copyright © 1969 by Review Publishing Co., Inc., Indianapolis, Indiana; for "Skiddley, Broadwaller, and the Pot of Gold," from Jack and Jill magazine copyright© 1974 by The Saturday Evening Post Company, Inc., Indianapolis, Indiana; for "Sasquatch: Creature of the North" from Sasquatch: Creature of the North and Other Mystery Stories, copyright © 1975 by The Saturday Evening Post Company. Originally appeared in YOUNG WORLD magazine, copyright © 1974 by The Saturday Evening Post Company.

Scholastic Magazines, Inc. for "Farthest West Village" by Lael Morgan. Reprinted by permission from Junior Scholastic, © 1974 by Scholastic Magazines, Inc.; for "Mysterious Monster of Murphysboro" by Virginia Sims. Reprinted by permission from Junior Scholastic, © 1974 by Scholastic Magazines, Inc.

John A. Sperry for the adaptation of "Ghost of the Lagoon" by Armstrong Sperry.

The Viking Press, Inc. for "The Money Machine." Adapted from THE MONEY MACHINE by Keith Robertson. Copyright © 1969 by Keith Robertson. By permission of The Viking Press.

womenSports Magazine for "Remembrance of Things Past" by Robert Hays. Reprinted by permission of womenSports Magazine, April, 1976.